PUBLIC SPEAKERS
YOU'RE NOT ALL THAT!

12 REASONS WHY EVENT PLANNERS WON'T HIRE YOU

(3400 + EVENT PLANNERS INTERVIEWED)

Orly Amor

Although the author and publisher have made every effort to ensure that the information in this book is correct at press time, the author and publisher do not assume and hereby disclaim any liability to any party for any loss, damage or disruption caused by errors or omissions, whether such errors or omissions result from negligence, accident or any other cause.

All rights reserved. No part of this book may be reproduced in any form or by any electronic or mechanical means, including information storage and retrieval systems, without written permission from the publisher or author, except in the case of a reviewer, who may quote brief passages embodied in critical articles or in a review.

ISBN-13:
Copyright © 2019 Orly Amor
All rights reserved

ACKNOWLEDGEMENTS

To my new friend, mentor, colleague and the person responsible for the idea behind the cover of this book, Leigh Simons. Thank you for coming into my life when you did, and I would have Sushi with you anytime. I am forever grateful.

***

To Berny and September Dohrmann, thank you for your support and encouragement to press on and follow my dreams. Thank you for the difference you make in people's lives and the difference you especially have made in mine. CEO Space is and will be for years to come my new home.

***

To Adam Markel, your generosity and guidance to accomplish one of my Bucket List items of getting to a TEDx talk is something I am and will be forever grateful for. Thank you for being a part of my life.

***

To Bert and Alexa Oliva and team. Thank you for your continued support for so many years. Thank you for bringing me into your home and into your family. I will love and cherish you for the rest of my days. Friends like you are a rarity.

***

To Victor Antonio Gonzales and Bill Walsh, thank you for your mentorship and support throughout my career as a Public

Speaker. I will never be able to thank you enough.

***

To my clients. You are the reason I do what I do and this book is mostly dedicated to you as you are making a difference in this world and as we accomplish the goal of impacting 200 Million people around the planet by 24 April 2025, remember you are a part of the bigger picture. It is as a unit that we will accomplish this goal and I am so grateful for you in my life.

***

To my husband Alex, thank you for your continued support and patience while I pursue my dreams. You have been my rock and I am forever grateful.

***

To all my friends, colleagues and acquaintances, there are too many of you to name one by one. I am so blessed to have you in my life, and I am forever grateful for your support and belief in me. This lifepath I have chosen could not have been achieved without you.

Orly Amor

CONTENTS

Acknowledgements ii

Introduction By Bill Walsh vii

Foreword By Berny Dohrmann 1

Prologue By Chris Adams 7

A Letter To You From The Author 15

1 Ready To Get Started? 21

2 The Most Common Question Of All 25

3 Why You Should Listen To Me? 27

4 Myths About The Industry 31

5 Public Speaking Is Not For Everyone 37

6 Assuming About Public Speaking 39

7 The Store Analogy 41

8 Contacting Event Planners Vs Cold Calling? – Both Are A Pain. 43

9 There Are No Seasons In Public Speaking 45

10 The Difference Between A Media Sheet And A Speaker Sheet 49

11 Who Do You Listen To? 55

12 When Event Planners Don't Respond? 59

13 Get Over Yourself! It's Not About You! 63

14 Pay To Play 65

15 Why Should I Keep Learning Public Speaking? I Have Been Speaking For Years. 69

16 "You Want Me To Book You? Have You Lost It Man?" 71

17 Coach Vs Mentor	75
18 Why Mental Toughness Is Needed To Succeed In Any Business And Especially In Public Speaking?	79
19 10 Tips You Need To Know Before Starting A Speaking Business	81
20 Biggest Mistakes I See Public Speakers Making	83
21 Facts About The Business Of Public Speaking	85
22 Where Can You Start Getting Aid Gigs?	89
23 The Admiral's Spiesthe Admiral's Spies	91
24 Let's Get To The 'Brass Tacks' – Making Money In This Industry	109
Conclusion	113
Resources I Resources To Find Speaking Opportunities	115
Resource - Ii	117
Here Are Some Of The Best Motivational Quotes That You Might Want To Read When You Feel Down, Discouraged Or Disappointed.	117
Resource- Iii What Type Of Speaker Are You?	121
Resource – Iv Recommended Readings For Self-Development And Encouragement	123
Resource – V Places You Can Get Coaching Clients And Get Invited To Speak Or Get Referred Speaking Gigs	125
Resource – Vi Companies In The Usa That Hire Speakers	129
My Gifts To You	143
About The Author	145

INTRODUCTION
BY BILL WALSH
America's Small Business Expert
Founder & CEO of Powerteam International

Public speaking is an art form! The quality of your communication will dictate the quality of your life!

What you will love about this book is that it breaks down everything you need to know to become a successful speaker & get booked on stages. Orly has not only been on global stages but she has also hosted speakers on her own stages in multiple cities per year. I love her presence & energy to always overdeliver. Always partner with the best in class!

When you empower your public speaking you will change the way you walk, talk as well as how you show up for any business meeting for the rest of your life. I have delivered over 5000 presentations to groups as small as 10 and as large as 25,000 over the past 20 years. I have seen it all in the world of public speaking. I will say it is not an easy industry to get started in or get to the top in.

My words are simple - BE AUTHENTIC from the stage.

As you read this book you will understand why it is so important to remain congruent to your message. You will have to weather the storms that every speaker faces! The reward is worth everything you will endure in becoming a world class platform speaker.

As for promoters and speaker site memberships - I would highly recommend you learn some of the secrets in this book so you have vast knowledge of what works and what does not. You will learn that on the way up in the speaker industry it is important you understand many of the rules. The concept of just getting booked to speak because you are great at something is a long way from the truth. Many of the best speakers in the world are always marketing!

Once you have completed at least 100 presentations in front of a live audience – only then have you just started your professional career as a speaker. I know that for more than a decade Orly has been helping experts make money from the stage. Always remember you don't have to be great to start but you have to start to be great!

Orly - Keep up the Great Work!

Bill Walsh
America's Small Business Expert
Top 30 Business Guru's in the World Guru Magazine
www.billwalsh360.com
www.ipowerteam.com

FOREWORD
BY BERNY DOHRMANN
Best Selling Author, Speaker, Mentor

You May Be All "That" And Even "More":

Having Coached the premier leading SPEAKER income earners of all time in my life time - Zig Zigler, Warner, Tony Robbins, of The Giant Within, Walt Disney, Bucky Fuller, Earl Nightengale, Jack Canfield of *'Chicken Soup'*, Sharon Lechter of *'Rich Dad Poor Dad'*, Bill Walsh of *Power Teams*, Greg Reid of *Secret Knock* and over 20 best sellers worldwide including *'Three feet from Gold'*, George Fraiser, John Grey of Mars and Venus Fame, and far too many to name them all here, well buddy Michael Gerber and E-Myth, smile, had to sneak Bob Proctor with 1.5 billion copies sold for *'The Secret In'*, like the Farmers Insurance Advertisement ...we know a thing or two in the *'Speaker Space'*.

Orly, as one of our http://www.ceospaceinternational.com Alliance Partners, transforms speakers' futures. As the MENTOR to the top Tier MENTORS, I value truth. I value no time-wasting bullshit. I value tools, real tools. I value tactics, real tactics. The Meat. The Potatoes that any budding speaker can now use to triple their income and double their time off. But HOW. Really HOW?

Triple Your Income…. Double Your Time Off:

Why listen to me? Well, my new smash best seller you've heard about or read about *'Super Change'* - the new AGE we reside within, sets the stage. The firm I founded and in which Orly is on faculty is known as *'CEO Space International'* – a four - decade mature outfit serving 150 nations to grow businesses (yours) faster and ranked 2010 - 2020 (ten years in a row) as the # 1 Press ranked Business Acceleration Conference in the world today. Forbes has ranked me a *Top Ten Keynote Global Public Speaker* and none of the Super Stars I named here made the *Top Ten List…* not one. Orly has access to every top-level speaker in the world today and why did she ask "me" to write the foreword? Because the majority of the *Multi-Million Dollar* speakers - chose to give back and mentor at *CEO Space* since the 1980's to today worldwide. We serve the TOP of the speaker leadership; having helped them to win and keep them winning over time. THAT IS our WHY. We have helped more speakers reach success than all other programs combined into one. Press ranked # 1. Orly chose the leader and it is pure JOY to shout out for ORLY's break through solutions for speakers across the world.

Due to my own reach of hundreds of millions of readers worldwide, this work of Orly's is a milestone in the Super Changing marketplace of raising up the career path of a professional speaker. The job of growing a speaking BUSINESS and BRAND is changing so fast you need a manifesto to know the steps to take. Just a SPIT into a floor spittoon ago, there was no fax, no smart phone or iPad; there was no digital or YOUTUBE or digital buyers and buying. Today everyone you know, everything you have read, everything you have studied is as obsolete as Speakers traveling on horseback were impacted by a Model T Ford. Today you are the MODEL T FORD and Orly is the STARSHIP ENTERPRISE as to what comes NEXT

IN GROWING A SPEAKING "BUSINESS" AND SUPER BRAND – something that works and that lasts over time.

Why? Simple. 5G. Orly wrote tools and tactics for the new 5G Super Change Markets in digital buying of speakers becoming the new normal. Now short is more. Less is best. And powerful Clips drive buying. Today everything will upgrade into 5G with over 4 Billion Devices rolling over the next 24 months - an industry in itself. Every speaker must become the leading edge in the Super Changing Speakers' FUTURE 5G Market Space. This means upgrading your smart phone, pads, computers, and internet of things; this means upgrading your web site as well as your social and all touch points to your buyers. Today the world of SPEAKERS IS SUPER CHANGING as never before. Orly presents the future today for speakers to grow SUCCESS NOW without unwanted delays and detours.

Orly presents the double line in the FAST TRACK EXPRESS lanes of CELEBRITY BRAND BUILDING, to our readers so YOU will never be stuck in the commuter lanes jammed to a speaker career stop. No economic ramp up in sight? Orly "IS" the next generation 5G upgraded Speaker GPS to those speaker economic ramp ups – brace yourself!

Orly is so good that she takes you step by step through the 12 SPEAKER HELL traps no one ever educates you to avoid - she detours you around each HELL TRAP with tools and tactics to arrive into speaker economic heaven. Orly's Speaker Economic ramp ups are just too many …….

Building a multimillion dollar speaking success in the market today has never been easier and never faster. It also has never been harder if you lack the 5G upgraded Speaker GPS to navigate the Super Changing landscape. The old books and models DO NOT WORK - have you learned THAT YET? In the all new Super Changing 5G world of speaking, the tips on what works, on what gives you tactical and proven modeling to win, are all in one publication. None of this work is HARD. All the steps are JUST NEW. Every reader will say ...if I had only known.

Personally, I have realized so many millions of dollars myself from the principles of Orly's leading edge next generation speaker BIBLE. I cannot recommend enough this work to the tens of thousands of speakers we support at CEO SPACE worldwide. Buy ten copies and gift this book to speakers you know and every time you're on stage give a copy of the PRINCIPLES to other speakers - with a signed note to keep you in mind in talks they are booking in the future. They will do the same....

How to Use – You're Not All That (Yet But You Soon Will Be)?

Buy ten copies and give this book to every speaker you meet. The pass along referral will inventory new talks gift givers win and those who don't won't.

When you are down to five or you're out, buy five more for inventory. Make it your GAME PLAN. Share winning.

Read this action-packed workbook the following way to *'Think and Grow Rich'* having grown up on Napoleon Hill's lap folks:

1. Underline with marker pen - review and highlight information you must ACT UPON.
2. Make notes to yourself in the margin in key ACTION to do listing.
3. Have a YELLOW PAD ENTITLED "THINGS TO DO LIST" and number and itemize things to do from the read.
4. 72 hours after completing - read your THINGS TO DO LIST and prioritize the flow that best works for you to

GO into your best future.
5. Do the work - the one cost too great to PAY is simply for speakers to DELAY. Trust me on that concept.

DO IT NOW is your rule. Say it in your mind. NEVER PAY THE FANTASTIC COST OF DELAY. Your future can simply not afford your delay to your own higher pay.

This work is the largest PAY RISE of any speaker's life today. 2020 -2050 is not your GRANDMOTHERS SPEAKER MARKET PLACE in full on SUPER CHANGE. Everything is TOOLS and everything is TACTICS. Speakers fail because they have weak plans, weak teams and lack resources required to win. Speakers win and win big because they have stronger plans, improved teams and elevated resources to cross the million-dollar finish line. If you earn a million or more today, earn tens of millions or 100's of millions more, like Tony. We both teach that when you reach your dream adopt a BIGGER DREAM. THINK BIG. It costs so little to THINK BIGGER. Bigger. BIGGER THAN THAT.

Orly will teach you to LIVE BIG by BEING BIGGER in the marketplace. Celebrating your genius in the marketplace is a strategy - a step by step, no accidents about it. Nothing left to luck or to chance. YOU ARE WINNING BECAUSE YOU ARE A WINNER WHO DID THE WORK TO WIN. That is your WHY. Money follows work.

Economics in any industry is unforgiving when you err. Napoleon Hill defined in *'Think and Grow Rich'*, that one had to decide as a non-drifter what they wished to DO and had to stay on course. Then Napoleon Hill drew a line in the sand and defined that YOU then must DO THE WORK to acquire the specialized knowledge current to your industry today. Shoes for horses may be in decline when everyone is moving on wheels. Be in the right time. Know the specialized knowledge in your current industry to the future unfolding in Super Change. Orly gives speakers the GPS to drive by and all that is required is you TURN INTO YOUR OWN BETTER SUCCESS.

Personally, I've made so many millions from the tactics in this book I just can't not recommend it to any speaker, from the new who are just starting to the VETS AT THE TOP in my own tribe I've mentioned here - READ 'YOU'RE NOT ALL THAT'. Take Orly and Bible up with you. Invite ORLY TO SPEAK at your events as the most important speaker to help in the world today....as that next speaker who is inspired and blessed to go all the way into your best possible future. Orly and Adam Markel host live Speaker Camps that frankly I feel are another value every Speaker must explore as well.......

Orly lives for that...only that...and it is her GINORMOUS HEART for Speakers that reminds me of Les Brown and Lisa Nichols, who give their lives away to that next soul lifted and supported. For SPEAKERS ORLY IS THE ONE...the only ONE. Trust ORLY as if your future depended upon her.... because folks....it truly does.

Berny Dohrmann
Author Super Change
Founder CEO SPACE INTERNATIONAL

PS: *I'm never having less than ten copies myself and I'm giving this book to every speaker I meet and this is global and endless every single year...you're next. Have a MULTI MILLION DOLLAR FUTURE as those you serve are crying out...yesterday is already too late for your solution to reach their lives.......*

PROLOGUE
BY CHRIS ADAMS
REAL ESTATE INVESTOR AND ENTREPRENEUR

After a grueling four-day seminar in San Diego, California I turned to Orly and said, "I know you're going to do great things." My name is Chris and I am a successful entrepreneur. I met Orly and I sat next to her at a convention where there were about 2,000 attendees and a dozen amazing presenters and motivational speakers.

We immediately became good friends and spent time talking about our past experiences, relationships and business dealings. Being an entrepreneur has its ups and downs like anything else. Orly shared her passion for The Law of Attraction and how she could manifest anything into her immediate reality. As I listened to her and got to know her better, it was obvious she was meant to follow her passion of helping people all over the world.

The conference and our mutual businesses revolved around real estate and how to flip properties. I could see that Orly's heart was excited about learning, yet she and I knew we were not going to put this into practice.

On the first day of the conference the host announced that they will be choosing three people from the audience to sing karaoke. All the participants needed to do was to sign up and choose a song from a predetermined list.

The singers were to perform on the last day of the conference. Orly turned to me and said, "I would love to be on that stage. I have my own backup music CDs with me." I replied almost immediately, "There will be many people on that list, and they are only choosing three." She responded, "Yeah, you're probably right. Chances are slim."

On the fourth day of the conference as they called the first singer and then the second singer to the stage, both of whom were very good, there was applause acknowledging their courage to go up on stage.

Orly disappeared for a few minutes. When she got back, she put her digital camera in front of her - I thought maybe she would like to have a couple of souvenir pictures, as this conference really was emotionally draining yet very inspiring. She turned to me and said, "Just in case I go on that stage, can I show you how this camera works?" I replied, "Sure, did you put your name in?" I asked, surprised by her request. She said "No, but just in case, I spoke to the MC and he said he would check."

I could not believe what I had just heard - she went directly to the source? The next thing we heard was the MC over the microphone state, "Where is Orly, that smiling young girl? Where are you Orly?" Orly jumped out of her seat and shouted, "Right here!"

The next thing I knew she was on stage singing and I was filming and taking pictures of the whole thing. The crowd was on their feet, clapping their hands. Orly was on all the big projector screens so everyone could see her. Everyone was dancing and clapping, and the MC had a smile from ear to ear, proud to have chosen her. I did not know what came over me, but I just started tearing from joy, like a proud father.

When Orly came back to her seat and the excitement subsided, I turned to her and said, "How did you do it? How did you get that MC to let you on the stage without signing up?" Her reply was, "Chris, I told you that I wanted to be on that stage from the moment they announced it. I also listened to you when you said there would be many people on that list. I did not let that stop me from envisioning me on that stage. I just called on the universe to show me how, then I listened to the answer and I seized the opportunity.

When the MC was by himself next to the DJ booth, I went to see him, and I knew I had about thirty seconds of his attention. I told him I sing, that I have my own CD musical back up and that if he lets me on that stage, he won't be disappointed. I told him he would be a hero and he would be fulfilling one of my own dreams which was to sing in front of a large crowd. That's it. Proving again, that the Law of Attraction works."

For those of you who don't know what the Law of Attraction is, there is a book called The Secret by Rhonda Byrnes, and many books have been written about the subject where like attracts like and hence the likelihood of great things happening to happier and more positive people as opposed to sad and more negative people.

The Speech

"Thank you so much, that was an awesome speech," one woman said. "Thank you so much! I can't wait to go home and start applying what I learned today," another woman added. "You are wonderful, I loved your energy as soon as I saw you," a third woman said excitedly. "Wow, your enthusiasm is contagious, thank you for sharing and inspiring all of us," another audience member stated while wiping her tears of joy.

This was the crowd gathering around Orly after she gave her first motivational speech. Overwhelmed by her speech and story, people felt compelled to let her know how much she had changed their lives in such a short period of time. Many of them were wondering if she was going to write a book about her experiences. I was also thinking, "Why not, why shouldn't Orly write a book?"

Earlier that morning, Orly woke up and looked around her house for some inspiration to start the day. One of her morning rituals was to go around the house and read the yellow Post-Its with their pretty flower linings, where a few of her favorite affirmations were written in black Sharpie, so that she could see them from anywhere in the house.

Then looking at the pool, in her Florida home she saw a frog swimming to find his way out. "That frog," she thought, "is me," wondering how she was going to come out of this speech in front of a few hundred people. "What if they don't like me? What if they don't think what I say is valuable to changing their lives?"

After hearing all the applause and testimonials to those exact fears, Orly realized that she was on the right track to fulfilling her mission.

As an attendee and a friend of Orly's for a couple of years, I thought again, "She needs to write a book about all of this."

After leaving the event on that September night, Orly and I got into the car and after a few moments of silence, as I predicted, Orly asked, "So what did you think?" In my mind I thought it was a perfect time to suggest writing the book, so I said, "Well, you heard them. They loved you." Not satisfied with my answer as I knew she wouldn't be, Orly replied, "Yes I heard them, but I want to know your opinion."

Orly likes to get to the point and gets annoyed if you don't. Knowing that and knowing not to give my opinion unless asked for, I was happy she asked. "I think you should write a book. I think you should tell your story. I think you should practice what you preach and pay it forward," I said with conviction. Orly's reply was immediate. "Me? Write a book? I don't know the first thing about writing a book. Where do I start? How do I know if people would want to read my book? And what makes me so different than any other book or story out there?"

Like I said earlier, I had known Orly for a couple of years, so I asked her, "How did all this start for you? How did you come up with a way to overcome all those challenges in your life?"

So here we were, both silently contemplating and then Orly responded, "Alright I'll do it, I will write a book that not only tells my story, but a book that when individuals read it, will make them feel I am beside them – they need to feel that I truly care about them and they need to have immediate results after reading the book. Fair enough?" I replied, "Fair enough. Let me know when it comes out."

What really happened? Then and Now.
In my own words. - Orly

The book that followed the above conversation was published in December 2017 on Amazon called 'The Twelve Powers We Hold Within – The Ultimate Paradigm Shift.'

May 2006, in Fort Lauderdale, Florida.

I'm a successful businesswoman. I own my own house and a beautiful BMW. I am a Property Management Consultant and a National Speaker on the subject of Residential Property Management for the last 10 years. I'm lounging on my Spanish terracotta - tiled pool deck. Beautiful clear blue skies. I watch a little frog struggling to climb out of the pool at the deep end. I start thinking, "this little frog wants to get out of his predicament just as much as I want to get out of mine. How can I get myself out of delivering my first motivational speech?"

I had been in property management for 16 years. For the past several years I had been speaking on that subject all over the country. My good friend, Connie, thought I was a natural in front of an audience. Six months prior, she asked me to give a speech at the women's shelter she was volunteering at. I refused!

She called me every day for three weeks asking if I had changed my mind. I finally asked, "Why me? There are many other speakers that speak on this topic?" She answered "I have known you for quite a while and you are a social magnet! People love you, you have great energy, you're successful and you are living the life most people can only dream about. I want you to share your story with us. YOUR WHOLE STORY."

What she wanted me to share is the following: I was a beaten up child, I was molested 4 times by different men before the age of 14, I was raped 3 times before the age of 22, twice gang-raped, left for dead, nine months apart, I was married to a very abusive men, both mentally and physically. As a result of that I had 4 abortions and I gained a morbid amount of weight, I was 428 pounds at my heaviest.

I gave my speech that day in front of a couple hundred people at the women's shelter with both employees and volunteers in the audience and when I was done there was not one dry eye in the room! I came out of hiding and I shared everything! The beatings, the molestation, the rape, the abusive husband . . . ALL OF IT.

After the speech, unlike other property management speeches, I was approached by women who thanked me, hugged me, and embraced me with such love and gratitude that I had never experienced before.
I remember one woman, in particular, who was in her early 40s. She had light skin, long auburn hair and beautiful green eyes. She came up to me crying profusely and said "Thank you, thank you!! You don't understand". I said, "yes I do understand, please calm down, everything is going to be ok." Back and forth we went until she yelled at me "NO, you don't understand." I was so taken aback it gave me goose bumps and I stood there in disbelief. Everyone around us froze and we were surrounded by silence.

She took a piece of paper out of her pocket and showed it to me while pointing with her index finger and said "this is how I was going to kill myself this morning! In fact, I don't even remember driving from my house to the shelter this morning. As you can see this is not where I was going. I heard you speak, and I now want to live. I just need you to show me how?"

I started crying and my thought was not "Wow, this is cool!" My thought was "Wow, I just saved someone's life!!"

This was the defining moment when I finally realized the power of no longer hiding my past and I discovered my true calling. I want to repeat living that moment for the rest of my life! That moment was so inspiring that I chose to have a career transition - into Motivational Speaking and Coaching.

So, here we are now. I am a business coach for public speakers because I want to impact 200,000,000 people around the planet by April 24th, 2025.

You can have it all - pain, fear, joy, love and you can choose to be happy. My intention is for you to share and not to hide. Have the courage because you never know whose life you're going to impact.

In that act of sharing there is contribution. You get to contribute to people's lives because they find themselves in your story and become courageous themselves.

No matter what you've been through. No matter what your story. Share your story, be a Mentor, become a public speaker because you may not know it now, but the life you save may never be able to thank you!

It is not by accident that you are reading this book. I hope to hear from you after you implement some of the tools, I give you here. So that we can change those lives together.

A Letter to You from the Author

Dear friend,

I have hired many coaches throughout my life, and I have learned that I do need a coach in every aspect of my life. At first it hurt my ego. I am educated and have achieved so many successes and have had so many accolades - who can help me better than me. Right?

Finally, I relented and hired an executive, business coach and he told me to write a mission statement for me. At first, I thought "is he crazy?" - a mission statement is for a business and I already have that. He continued to explain that if I didn't have a 'Definite Major Purpose' for my life that I was wasting away in the rat race called Life.

I took that to heart, because up to that point, I had only thought of making money and traveling and living life on my terms. So much was taken from me that I got angry very quickly and was impatient. (I still am very impatient about certain things.)

When I realized that my purpose was bigger and it was not all about me, then things, people, circumstances and events were starting to shift around me as well.

As I pondered on this question of my 'Definite Major Purpose' I finally came up with the following:

"My Current Definite Major Purpose in Life

Is to glorify the Universe/Creator by becoming a Deca Millionaire as an Author, Public Speaker and Mentor in order to provide well for my family and give generously to charities, and to be able to help others and teach others across the world (being an internationally known speaker) what I have learned in the process."

Take a moment and think about what you do and why you do it. Make a list of why you want to make money doing it as well. This list will get you through the tough times. This has nothing to do with finding your WHY or Visualizing where you want to be. This is hard core. It will give you a sense of direction.

As if my 'Definite Major Purpose' was not enough, I was now asked to say what I was willing to give in return for the realization of my Purpose. I thought my coach was joking. I asked, "to give whom? Who is helping me? And how do I know what to give back?"

My coach insisted that I was not thinking big enough. He asked, "What is your real intention on how you will operate and from what place of service, to your family, community, city, country, and the world? You are here to serve, in case you lost that in our conversation. Think about it."

I really had to Get Real and Be Real with myself and I realized what he was saying was not just some random message. I realized that I do have much to give and receive but most importantly my being alive here today is much bigger than what I was thinking.
After much thought here is what I came up with:

What I Intend to Give in Return for The Realization of This Purpose

"I intend to give excellent, honest and dependable service to my Mentoring clients, my partners, investors and affiliates. I will do even more than what I am going to do, and I will do it with a good attitude. I will go the extra mile; I will exceed expectations. I will "look for other people's interests and not just my own". I will work hard 6 days a week. I will utilize my gift of persuasion to bring as much business as I can to everyone I am associated with. I will continue educating myself perpetually so that I can become the best that I can be, and I will pass that knowledge on to friends, associates, students who want to learn my trade or from me recognizing their own inner beauty and gift. I will give back to the world and my community as I am guided spiritually. I will budget and keep my expenses modest (in comparison to my income) so as to be financially stable and free to give as much as possible to help others. I Will Be A Good Steward!!!"

Getting this done reminded me of the boy in the movie "HUGO" where he explains his purpose on this planet. "the world is a big machine and I exist because I am one of the parts of the machine that makes it work. If I did not exist, then the machine would not be able to work properly or would stop working all together." That was so profound for me that I took it a step further and decided on the plan that would help me achieve my 'Definite Major Purpose' and here it is:

"My Plan to Achieve My Definite Major Purpose is through: Networking – Collaboration - Influence"

My dear new friend, whether you are thinking about becoming a Public Speaker, whether you are just starting out as a Public Speaker or whether you are a Professional Public Speaker or

even a Veteran, I encourage you to think about these three components as a Stomping Ground. It is never too late to write, edit and revisit any of your Goals, Ambitions, Mission and 'Definite Major Purpose.'
Because if you want to change or impact this world it has to start with you first and foremost.

To Your Ongoing Success.
Orly

"When you find your purpose, it is like your heart has been set a light with passion. You know it absolutely, without any doubt."
– Orly Amor

1
READY TO GET STARTED?

I used to give a class called "Get paid to speak in Four Weeks or Less."

Since then times have changed tremendously and the industry as a whole has done 180 degrees when it comes to getting paid as a Speaker.

Lately everyone that loses their job or retires is now a Coach or a Public Speaker of some sort.

Still this industry is not going away any time soon and it's a business after all. There are many points that are important to know about this business and I want to give you some of the thoughts I had when I first started learning this industry and why this book is coming out now?

I had to ask myself some very hard questions that I did not know the answers to and needed to figure out:

1. **Before getting paid to speak you need to know a few things about yourself:**
   - What kind of Speaker are you?
   - Why you need to be speaking?
   - When and where to speak?
   - What are you willing to do?

- How do you get paid and how much?

2. **Signature Speech or a Good Packaged Message (Putting it together)** do you know if you are a good speaker or mediocre or Awesome? Which one do you want to be? If the answer is "The Best" then you need to know how to:

- Speak 'TO' not 'AT' the Audience
- The DOs and DON'Ts on Stage and off the Stage
- It's not delivery it's discovery, it is not what's on the outside but what is on the inside that counts
- "People don't care how much you know, until they know how much you care." – Jim Rhone

3. **Speaker Sheet vs Media Sheet, do you know the difference?**
- What is on it?
- What is their purpose?
- The way they are both useful.

4. **Does a Speaker need to Network?**
- Never say never – If you don't make enough money, you don't know enough people.
- "Your Network is your Net Worth."
- Just another Skill you need for your business of Public Speaking
- Very high ROI

5. **There are 7 Platforms in Public Speaking and You need to know:**
- How to choose which one?
- What is the difference between them?
- When are they looking for Speakers and how to

approach them?

6. **The Diva Syndrome:**
   - Not only public speakers have it and why it's important to know that?
   - What do event planners do with your Speaker Sheet?
   - How you behave before, during and after an event?

7. **Repeat Business is Best Business,** but you need to get there first. I say this all the time "Pay me now or pay me later" because you need to learn this business inside and out. Or you will need to go back to the drawing board and work harder to get there:
   - The art of Pay to Play. Yes, it is an art form only if you know the business of Public Speaking and have all the infrastructure to support it. Don't do it if you don't know it. It is very lucrative once you know how and when done strategically.
   - Are you a good Businessperson? Being an Entrepreneur is one of the hardest mindsets to have. You must be willing to sacrifice and do more than is expected and then some.

8. **Are you OPEN for Business?**
   - Read the Store Analogy
   - Do you have all the right forms?
   - Follow up or go to the bottom of the Totem pole

9. **I am in the business of Public Speaking Now What?**
   - NSA (National Speakers Association) and Speaker Bureaus
   - What is your Job?
   - How many kinds of Event Planners are there?

10. **If it's going to be, it's up to me.**
- Hiring VA vs doing it yourself
- Do I need a booking Agent?
- How fast can I get a Speaking gig?

11. **What about having a Coach?**
- A Public Speaking Coach (are you coachable?)
- A Content Coach
- A Delivery Coach
- They can be all in one and you need help in all three.

12. **I am a Rock Star Speaker. Really?**
- Who do you hang out with?
- Are you popular or busy?
- Are you living the Dream?

All these thoughts and all these questions I had to ask myself and learn on my own until I hired a coach. Once I hired a Coach I was humbled because what I was thinking about myself and what I knew - I was utterly wrong. I needed to be open to learning and be open minded to receive even straight up criticism. I thought I knew it all. I did not and I still don't know it all. Most of all I had to be hungry for it. It is a wonderful industry, but it is changing, and Super Change will affect it. Are you ready?

2
THE MOST COMMON QUESTION OF ALL

Here is the question I get every single day, multiple times a day by prospects and clients:

"So Orly, how do I get speaking gigs? Most tell me they don't pay, and some want me to sponsor my speaking and then sell my stuff (Products/Services.) What should I do?"

For the past five years I have interviewed over 3400 event planners that hire public speakers on a regular basis.

They all have answered the same way, almost verbatim. The way that I have chosen to share those answers with you are in this book. The event planners have been bombarded every day by speakers who just don't have it together and those who think they do, don't and have an attitude about it.

You might think by reading this, that this does not apply to you. Let's address that immediately. You don't need this book if:

- You are getting **paid** bookings 5-12 times a month with little or no effort (Some of you call it referrals);
- You are making above $200K a year from public speaking alone;
- You have a Product or Service that sells even if event planners refuse to let you sell from the stage; and if

➢ You are happy with your Public Speaking business.

We will cover all this in the book but if you're doing well then stop reading this book and give it as a gift to someone who really wants to learn or take their business to the next level.

"Through Your Greatest Pain, comes your greatest glory." – Mark Twain

3
WHY YOU SHOULD LISTEN TO ME?

Hi, my name is Orly Amor. Nice to meet you! I have been speaking on all kinds of stages for the past 23 years. At first, I was speaking all over the country on Property Management. That was my field of expertise from 1996 to 2011. In 2006, I started combining my efforts - speaking about my journey to self-empowerment and overcoming challenges of life through mindset mastery.

What is my background? I have a Law Degree and an MBA, and I am a Certified Behavior Analyst which means nothing in the world of Public Speaking, but I regress.

I also studied the Business of Public Speaking in 2010 and I am the Creator of The Business in a Box for Public Speakers. I would love to share this story as I do so often when asked how I got started being a Business Coach for Public Speakers.

I was speaking at a conference in Arlington, TX and at the breakroom for Speakers three guys/speakers approached me and one of them asked "aren't you Orly Amor?" I did not remember seeing or meeting this guy in my life, so I felt kind of embarrassed for not remembering. I said politely "I'm sorry do I know you? Have we met before? Because I don't remember." He replied "No, no, we have never met officially but I've seen you on the circuit." (The Circuit is referred to as the circle of

Speaking Platforms where you see most speakers appear.)

I was relieved and just kicked into Networking mode and we all just introduced ourselves, what we speak about, and shared anecdotes about certain events etc.

One of the guys finally asked "so Orly, I'm just curious, how did you get this gig?" I responded as if it was common knowledge "I don't know, I called, I told them what I speak about, they paid me and I'm here." They all looked at me as if I had three heads and said in unison "You got paid?"

Before I continue this story, I want you to know that until that moment I did not know Speakers spoke for NO FEE. Or as some of you would say for FREE. We will cover the difference in this book as well.

I responded in shock "Why, you didn't?" One of them responded with, "Well, we got our expenses paid but we did not get paid." I said without hesitation "Oh, no, I got paid and I got my expenses paid." They all said in unison again as if they rehearsed this "Well, we want to know how you did that?"

Now, you also need to know that until that time I had no coaching in mind for this industry and so I answered jokingly "Well if I tell you, I will have to charge you." And before I could say "just kidding." They all said "Ok, just name your price." I was floored. My mouth wide open and I was thinking 'What? What just happened? Are they crazy?'

Well, we continued talking about the industry where I knew a few facts and notions about the Speaker Sheet and Media Sheet etc. We had to go back as I was the next speaker, so we exchanged numbers and promised to stay in touch.

On my way back home so many thoughts were firing at me. Maybe that's what's missing in this industry? Maybe Speakers are broke because they just don't know how to treat this business of public speaking as a business. I sat at the airport for a couple of hours and really thought about what it is that I do, that makes me successful.

I also remembered a conversation with some of my peers a few years back where I was telling them that the average Public Speaker needs to be making a minimum of $150K a year. (Side note: I was tripling that in those days)

All my speaker friends laughed at me saying I was crazy, that some don't even make $30K, $50K, maybe $80K, $100K "You're crazy Orly, and $150K you're out to lunch Orly." I just calmly replied "ok, you do you and I'll do me. I know what I'm talking about." They laughed and I pushed it aside as if it wasn't important since they didn't want to listen.

Funny thing happened in June of 2017. The NSA (National Speakers Association) came out with an article that stated that the average public speaker needed to be making $177K a Year. I took that article and sent it to every one of my peers who had laughed at me back then.

All this brought me to study this industry and go deep into all the nonsense that was said about it and all the truths and all the myths.

4

MYTHS ABOUT THE INDUSTRY

Myth #1
You need a Website

I hear it all the time. "Let me call you back when I have my website." Are you kidding? Who knows about you to even go to your website? Don't get me wrong if you already have one – that's great; but if you don't - that's also great. That is not even where event planners go to find out about you. (I will cover where they go later) ..... It is also not where they go to hire you. I have had a website for so long and I have a form on my website through which they can start the hiring process and in 23 years, I have never gotten one single hire from my website. So, to those of you who want to continue your efforts and time on a Website before getting paid to speak.... continue.

Disclaimer: Some professional speakers who have been speaking for over 10, 20 or more years have a website that is producing them bookings and gigs. They also belong to a few Speaking Bureaus and have a dedicated agent for their businesses. They pay the Bureaus and Agents between 20% - 40% Commission and sometimes more. If you have the monetary bandwidth to do all this, once again – great! But know this, you must be already making $15K + per gig for any of these Bureaus and Agents to even look at you. If you don't make this amount on a regular basis, a few times a month, then continue reading. You're not all that!

Myth #2
You Need a Book

Let's face it, if you have a book, I congratulate you - it's awesome and a major accomplishment when done right. If you are an Amazon Published Author that's great and I am very proud of you as well. Unless you are a New York Times bestselling author, it's not such a big deal.

Furthermore, Bestselling means just that, Best Sales Made when you launched the book and it held that position for a few hours or days and then you got a badge from Amazon. That is awesome but it is now considered a Glorified Business Card and you will get some recognition in your Bio, but it will not get you booked to speak and will not guarantee the monetary compensation for speaking.

So, if you think You're All That, because you are an Amazon Published or Bestselling Author? Think again.

Myth #3
You need to have a Signature Talk

Unless you're giving a TEDx Talk, you don't need a signature talk. That is very Old School in Public Speaking. What you do need is a well formulated Message. I will talk about this later as well. In the old days, let's say 10 to 15 years ago, a signature talk was what we saw Tony Robbins, Les Brown and Lisa Nichols, to name a few, do. Tony talked about his one room apartment where he slept in the bathtub etc...., Les talked about how he was a Janitor at this radio station and one day the DJ was drunk and passed out so he seized the opportunity and took over, Lisa talks about her abusive relationship etc.... and of course they all came out on top and are doing great by inspiring and motivating us all.

Those days of the FEW Speakers hired all the time are gone. I do want to thank them for opening the doors to so many of us, so that WE continue the process of sharing our own stories and impacting lives. But you don't need a Signature Talk. What you need is to be recognized for your Message.

Some Speakers think they have that message well packed. They DON'T.

Myth #4
You need to have a following on Social Media

There is a huge difference between having a track record on social media called Social Proof and having followers on social media called Popularity.

It does depend on what you are using it for? Social Proof is necessary when your clients are looking at you. I have not much of that as I decided to do the least amount possible, because it took too much of my time. Now, and because of this book, I am doing a little more and hiring outside help.

The number of followers is only important when an event planner wants you to Sponsor the event and Pay to Speak on their stage so that you help promote the event and make the event planner look good with all the other speakers. But there is a downfall to that, and I will cover that later too. For now, it's just good food for thought.

Myth #5
You need to be a great Speaker

Let's get real, everyone started somewhere. Like Bill Walsh said, "Public Speaking is an art form." Therefore, you need to start somewhere. A good place to start is Toastmasters or hiring a Speaking Coach. (Or you can go to www.SpeakerTrainingBootCamp.com given by the Global Mentoring Center and or www.SpeakToEnroll.com given by More Love Media with Adam Markel and his team to help you with your TEDx talk. They are the best in the business.) You need to get trained on crafting and delivering a speech as well as practicing your speech in front of an audience and get real and professional feedback.

When I started in this business, I thought I was good and then I hired a coach who gave me a reality check about this craft.

His name is Victor Antonio. I saw Victor speak at a local event in Fort Lauderdale, FL. He was so dynamic, authentic, full of life and enthusiasm, I thought, 'wow he is awesome!' After seeing him speak at a couple of other events and taking one of his programs that involved group training, I asked Victor if he would take me under his wing and help me up my game in Public Speaking. He said he does not take any One on One clients.

I begged and pleaded and wanted to pay whatever he asked just to get him to mentor and coach me. He still refused, and said that he does not coach anyone individually because "they are all full of excuses to do the work and I have no time or patience for that," I told him that I am not like other people, I don't think I know it all and I will be his Poster Child if he just gave me a chance. If he said "jump" I will say "how high." He finally agreed and gave me a price that was pretty high, but I did not discuss, I just paid and we committed to when and where and what I need to bring him.

He asked me to bring a few videos of my speaking and all I had are a couple of DVDs from my Property Management Speaking Life. He opened his portable DVD player and played the DVD without sound and in fast forward mode. After about 15 seconds, he put his hands over his face and said, "oh my God Orly, that is terrible, so terrible."

At that moment I wished for floor would open as a big hole and swallow me into the earth. I felt my heart ripped into shreds and could not believe what I just heard. He went on to explain all the little things to watch for, my own body language and the audience's body language and so on. That was THE most humbling moment in my speaking career. I not only thought I was good, I thought I was a Bad Ass Speaker. I thought I knew what I was doing. So, thank you Victor Antonio for waking me up from my slumber and helping me begin my journey as a Professional Speaker.

"Experience isn't always the best teacher, evaluated experience is." – John Maxwell

5
PUBLIC SPEAKING IS NOT FOR EVERYONE

If you experience faint or nausea and perspire profusely before you speak in public, it's OK. You can learn to manage and get passed it.

With training, experience and practice, you can become better and better at this craft. There is always room for improvement. I still, after 23 years of public speaking, am looking to learn and grow and get feedback.

So, don't get caught up in the "I am not good at public speaking" and get out there as much as possible. Those of you who say "I have no problem in front of an audience, I have been speaking and giving trainings for a long time, I don't need training or feedback", think again, you're not all that and we all need improvement. We all need to work at this craft because we are all work in progress.

The most important advice I can give you in this context is: Don't Practice in Front of a PAID Audience.

If you want to master your craft, you can speak at Kiwanis, Lions Clubs, Score, Vistage and other organizations that will give you some stage time to get over your nervousness and maybe get some feedback.

Just remember and this is my Tag Line "If You Have A Message, someone is always willing to Pay for It."

6

ASSUMING ABOUT PUBLIC SPEAKING

You would be amazed as to how many speakers confuse the 'keynote' market with the 'seminar' market. And because of this, they have a hard time building their speaking business.

- They don't know the difference between a Speaker Sheet and a Media Sheet.
- They don't know the difference between a Lectern and a Podium, they interchange these words consistently.
- They think Speaking is a 'One and done.'
- They think because they have a TEDx talk they are automatically going to get booked and paid as a speaker.

It has taken me over nine years of coaching speakers, to realize that I am still learning and that I am still Not All That as a Speaker and why I crave feedback and learning different techniques from different Speakers like Adam Markel, Bert Oliva and others.

Let's cover some of these things that you must understand about the Business of Public Speaking.

7
THE STORE ANALOGY

Let's imagine for a moment that you and I are really good friends and we are going to open a brick and mortar store. So, let's agree on a few things before we decide on what we will be selling as it is irrelevant at this moment.

Ready to play along and imagine? I hope you said yes.

We need a location, and because we are so lucky we have an amazing real estate agent that found us the best location and space.

We need a key to the front door? Yes. We need the hours of operation on the door? Yes. We need the name of the store above the door on a nice sign? Yes. When we go inside, we need a cash register, a computer or iPad to process our Credit Cards? Yes. We need an alarm system and a video camera system? Yes. We need insurance for the store and a Liability insurance? Yes. And we need a bank account and a bookkeeper because you and I don't like that accounting job? Yes.

Did I mention what we will be selling in the store? NO!

Well that is the Business of Public Speaking. You need the right infrastructure or else you will not get hired. This is not the time to get ready, this is the time to BE Ready.

Hence the reason why Speakers don't get hired and we will cover that in the twelve reasons.

8

Contacting Event Planners vs Cold Calling? – Both Are a Pain.

F or most of us, cold calling is extremely unpleasant because you're uninvited, and they're busy, and you need something, and they don't. Ask yourself: Does anybody get up in the morning thinking, "Boy, I've got a very busy day today. I hope at least a dozen people call on me today trying to sell me stuff or set up appointments to sell me stuff."

Many will buy books and tapes that teach dozens of ways to bully, sleaze, and lie their way into their prospect's heads. But in the end, you are still an uninvited pest. Not fun to be with and not fun to have to deal with. Is it any wonder that your prospects are always "out" or "in the shower"?

In Public Speaking it is the same with Prospecting and reaching out to Event Planners. They get hundreds if not thousands of calls and/or emails a day. And you think you're special? Think Again.

Because cold calling/prospecting is so unpleasant, most salespeople/Speakers devise dozens of time-wasting techniques to avoid doing it. Meticulous activity logs. Endless "research" on the Web. "Networking" or should I say gossip calls with other struggling friends. Calling people, you know will be unavailable, and not leaving a voice mail. Filling out time management tools. Counting their paperclips and organizing their office. (Don't laugh, it happens all the time!).

Does this approach make a person better? Does it benefit the prospect/Event Planner? Anyone? What's missing?

If you've been following my Blogs, you must have read that there are 64,000 events a DAY in America alone that pay Public Speakers. Yet if you are struggling, maybe it's your approach. I have seen hundreds of Speakers write long emails to event planners who obviously are too busy to read. But more importantly the Speaker does not know if they are contacting the right person.

So, let me simplify this for you. Make sure it's the right person first.

9

THERE ARE *NO* SEASONS IN PUBLIC SPEAKING

If you are anything like me, you are tired of hearing from potential clients only 'after the holidays or after the New Year'. In my head I am always intrigued by that "Do people just stop working between Halloween and the 2nd of January? or during the Summer after 4th Of July?" and one other thought comes to mind " People do not make money and or pay their bills during those seasons?" I bet you anything that those are just excuses.

Well, in Public Speaking there are no seasons. One of my clients, Joe, who had hired me at the end of April was so excited about the process and what he learned that he did the program within Six Weeks. (The Program is 12 Sessions not 12 Weeks, so I encourage my clients to go as fast or as slow as they like.)

In the beginning of June, he called to let me know that he was going on vacation with his family for a week and would resume when he got back. Once he was back, he called to let me know that he would begin contacting event planners after the summer because most people would be on vacation and he would probably have no luck in booking gigs. I said very firmly "Joe, there are no seasons in Public Speaking and since my contract promises you will make a minimum of $150K in your first year in Public Speaking, you can't take the summer off." He responded, "so I better get to work then?" I said "Yes."

Towards the end of July, I got a call from Joe. "Orly, I am so excited - you will never believe what happened. I emailed and called over 729 Places so far and got 298 responses and I have already obtained three bookings for the end of August and a couple for September and now I am getting 10-15 Responses a day." I simply said, "and you wanted to take off for the summer?" He replied "I know right? Boy I was wrong, and I get it now, back to work I go."

For you the reader, let me ask you this. If you had a store would you close it during the holidays or the summer because most people were out of town? I bet you that the answer to that would be NO. So why would the business of Public Speaking be any different?

As I said before, there are two reasons why Public Speakers are broke or making less than $100K a year.
1. It is because they don't know how this business works and we can't blame them for that. They don't know what they don't know.
2. They are lazy and just don't want to do the work. That's It.

My suggestion is - learn this business like any other business and give it your 100% for a full year, that is 365 Days and then you will really be able to take off whenever you want.

You call yourself a Specialist, Expert, Master, Guru, or even an Icon, which is great but now everyone says they are, so who do we believe? The one that shows up as an Authority in their field of expertise. They walk their talk and don't need to say they are the best. They simply ARE!

Merry Christmas and Happy New Year. I wish for you all what

you wish for yourself and more. Health, happiness and lots of Speaking Gigs in the years to come!

10

THE DIFFERENCE BETWEEN A MEDIA SHEET AND A SPEAKER SHEET

Yes, there is a big difference. Both are talking about you, but the media sheet is glitzy and focusing on you, whereas the speaker sheet is more business-like and focusing on the event planner. Let's talk about the Media Sheet and its purpose and next we will cover the Speaker Sheet.

The Media Sheet

The Media sheet, the Speaker Sheet and the Press Kit are often confused, and the terms are used interchangeably. They are very different from one another and are used for different Purposes.

Let's get the Press Kit out of the way as it is just a way to get the pages of your website into a document that represent an overall of 'Who you are? and What you do?' in a concise and precise way like an Article in a Magazine.

The **media sheet** shows what you have done and where you have been **featured**. For example, you were featured in a podcast or in a blog. Maybe you were featured in a magazine or you were on TV, CNN, NBC, or Fox. For a public speaker, the media sheet contains the topics on which you speak, but it is more visually interesting.

The media sheet is what you use to get more **media exposure** — to add to your media sheet. You get podcasts, magazines, TV appearances, etc. because you already have some experience with those forms of media. If you are just starting out and don't have a lot of media experience yet, the sheet then, contains information on you and what you speak about, with your picture and maybe your logo at the top. You may also add logos of associations you belong to, like Lions Club, Kiwanis or The ABC Association for Architects. Even though you think it is not relevant because you are a New Speaker, it is for now, relevant.

This sheet is visually attractive and very aesthetic. It is designed to get you noticed and help create more opportunities to increase public awareness of you and your topics. A good thing to put on a Media Sheet is any Cover of Books or CD program you have for purchase. Media outlets are looking for the Expert with a Solution to a Problem. And if your Book, Product or Service can solve that problem they may call you for an interview.

The Media Sheet is not good for getting booked as a Public Speaker. Event planners don't care about the Aesthetics of your Media Sheet, the numerous Media Outlets you were featured on and all the other organizations you belong to. It does not serve their purpose, which is to bring a Speaker that will deliver the Solution to a Problem or will bring something Fresh or New to their Conference or Event that they never had before.

Let me share this:
Remember my story with the three speakers in Arlington TX? Here is what happened next. During our conversation about getting paid to speak, we were talking about the industry and

the following are some of the highlights of that conversation.

I asked one of them to show me his Speaker Sheet and he said, "what is that?" I thought "oh boy, here goes." "Do you have a flier or something you show Event Planners to get Booked?" He said, "Oh, a Media Sheet?" I said, "That will do." He gave me an 8.5x11, 4-page folded flier printed on glossy beautiful quality paper. As I was looking it over for about ten seconds I said, "This is Garbage!" He was so insulted and replied with a "What do you mean? I paid over Five Hundred Dollars to get this done by a professional."

I responded, "I understand that, but it goes directly to the Garbage, the Event Planner does not even look at your name before it hits the Garbage can."
I continued "You see there was a Survey done of the 100 Most Stressful Jobs in America. Number One was Military/Jet Fighter Pilot, Number Five was Event Planner. (according to the survey of March 2019 by ABC. Event Coordinator/Planner is now at number 6) Do you actually think that they have the time to Read all that you have put into this Four Page Flier? Do you think they have the time to look at where your topics and the information to contact you are? The answer is No. How about simplifying their life? You've heard of 'Less is More' right?" I gave him a couple of pointers and we exchanged numbers and we all had to go back to the Conference Hall.

Speakers need to know their audience, and more importantly you need to know who you're serving. The answer is 'The Event Planner.' What is it that you can contribute to making their life easier?
The Media Sheet has its purpose and only one, To Get You More Media Exposure.

The Speaker Sheet

Let's look at the Speaker Sheet, its purpose and the science behind it.

The Speaker Sheet contains much of the same information as the media sheet, except for all the media-based items. There is no need for them, as event planners are not as impressed by the fact that you were on Fox News or the cover of the Huffington Post magazine. They just don't care about the fact that you met Sr. Richard Branson or Oprah.

What the event planner needs to know is:

- How are you going to make them look good?
- How are you going to help them be the hero of the day of their event?
- How are you going to serve their audience (while making them look good)?

Resuming my Story of how it all began:

After that Conference in Arlington my trip back to NY was a grueling 16 hours of layovers and delays. I was stunned as there was no rain or snow - all mechanical problems with the plane. I thought 'that's comforting'!

That's what the event planner is looking at. They want to see what your topics are of course, and what the audience will get out of it, but that information is usually on a media sheet. On a speaker sheet you just list the topic. If the planner is not interested in the topic, they're not going to hire you. They may ask you for what's in it for the audience, but until they're excited about the topic themselves, they won't hire you.

Your Title

The speaker sheet needs to have the information and should also include your Title. What is your title? Who are you?

I am a business coach for public speakers, but my title is actually how event planners recognize the ultimate results they can expect. With me, the ultimate result is that I'm the ultimate paradigm shifter. That's my title. For some people it means something, and for others it means absolutely nothing.

The title depends on what market you are going after as well. I'm going after public speakers. I'm going after coaches. The title also depends on who your target audience is. The event planner, however, doesn't care who your target audience is, they just want to know what your title is. It's exciting to them. If the event planner can sell/market you, they're happy. It's always a challenge for an event planner to think, "*Well how am I going to sell/market this Speaker? How am I going to sell/market Him/Her/Them to my audience?*" Right?

Also, on a speaker sheet, you want to have a couple of things that do give you credibility. Maybe a logo, or if you have one, the cover of your book. The speaker sheet should also have your picture, or headshot.

"Appetizer" Placement

All of these elements are important, but they also have to be at the right place on the speaker sheet. It's all about placement. Have you been to a restaurant lately? When you open the menu, what is on the left-hand side? The appetizers and/or drinks. Do you know why? The normal analogy that people come up with is that we read from left to right and you usually start with an appetizer or a drink. But the real reason? The Restaurant makes more money selling those items.

It's the same principle on your speaker sheet. What does the event planner need to know right away about this speaker that is intriguing and inviting and marketable for them?

Both the media sheet and the speaker sheet are needed in the business of public speaking. There's a science behind it that you must understand in this business, or else you're sending out things that are probably not getting noticed. The sheet must be nice and clean and tight with certain things in certain places.

Some speaker sheets don't even get looked at. Why is that?

The information about the speaker is not there. Some people actually *forget to include their phone number on the sheet*, or the phone number is in such small font that the event planner doesn't see it, so it goes into the garbage or gets deleted.

There is too much that the event planner needs to read. What many speakers do is combine the speaker and media sheets into one document. For the event planner, it can be overwhelming to read so — you guessed it — into the garbage it goes. If presenting your information is that complicated, then you are most likely complicated as a speaker and the event planner may not want to work with you.

The moral of this section is. **Plan both your media and speaker sheets with care.**

11
Who do You Listen To?

I get asked this a lot. "Orly, I have been through so many programs and online courses and signed up for this, that and the other. Now I am listening to you and I also like what I hear. But whom should I listen to?"

I think we all have a good message and good intentions. Yes we have gone through our own process to have the success we earned till this point. But if you hire anyone, and you don't do the work they tell you to do then it won't work, no matter who you hire and what program you bought. There is no Magical Formula, this is a Business and unless you understand that and really get it, you won't succeed.

Here is a self-promotion statement but it is used to make a point. "I am the only one in the world that Promises you will make a minimum of $150K your first year in Public Speaking and I put it in Writing." That means that after I build your infrastructure and position you for this industry and you start the process of getting booked and after a year of following my process to the Tee and did not make the Minimum, (and you can prove it of course) I will work with you until you do or work with you another Year at no charge. This is how much faith I have in my process. Let's not kid ourselves, any monies made from Public Speaking is considered money coming from Public Speaking. So even after a Year if you HAD NOT done the process to the tee, you will not make it.

I have hired many coaches at one point or another and I love them all. I bought their book or their program or I am a part of the ongoing group or mastermind and you know of them or have hired them. If you did not do or implement what you learned, how do you know if it works or not?

"People give business to and refer business to people they know, like and trust." – Bob Burg

Before hiring a coach for any part of your life:

- Be ready and open to receive the information
- Read the fine print of the contract and ask questions if any arise.
- Ask for references
- And then make sure you listen to your gut. Do you like the person you're about to hire?
- Think about it, if there was a problem or a challenging situation. Will you be able to be open and honest with your coach to find a resolution?
- Are you stubborn? Or are you coachable?

I say the following jokingly, but I want to make a point. "We are all adults and vaccinated." Meaning you need to take responsibility for all of your actions and decision making and learn from them or move on.

Sometimes you can buy an item online or at the store and when you get home it's not as good as you had expected and therefore you either return it or you keep it because it's cool anyway and you learned your lesson.

Some of the programs are very lucrative - if you are going to invest in yourself (as you should: 10% of your annual income should go into self or business development) or in a business, it's the same thing.

You need to do the work and give it a minimum of one year so that you can go through the four seasons before you judge any program.

Before you give up or judge and criticize, like most of the people I meet, ask yourself the question "Did I give it my hundred percent?" If the answer is No. Go back to the drawing board.

I live by a very popular philosophy *"To Know and Not to Do, Is Not to Know at All."* – Leo Buscaglia
(Original proverb by Laozi and later also used by Stephen Covey.)

You may think you know a business inside and out. But unless you have worked in it full time for Ten Thousand Hours or a couple of years, you don't know this business.

Also, things change, industries change, people change - are you willing to be flexible with the changes or do you want to keep doing the same thing over and over expecting different results? That is called insanity. You've heard this before? Right?

The moral of this chapter is, hire whomever you like, invest in yourself/in this business, do everything at a hundred percent effort and consistency and then decide to stay or to move on.

12
WHEN EVENT PLANNERS DON'T RESPOND?

Earlier on I wrote about how stressful event planners are and what happens to them daily.

Think about this. They have an event to plan and it consists of the following:

- Clients
- Venues
- Sponsors
- Vendors
- Employees
- Volunteers
- Program
- Scheduling
- Speakers

In between all of these elements they have to cater to their own wellbeing, family and social life if they have one. They have to answer phone calls, emails and have meetings with clients, sponsors, vendors and team. Guess when they have time to answer your email? When I say you're not all that, I mean no disrespect, but I have a lot of compassion and understanding for Event Planners because I am one of them as well. I hold two conferences a year, one on land and one on a cruise ship and I have another company where we host over 30 events a year. So, I get it!

What can you do when event planners don't respond? Be patient. Contact many and don't hold your breath till they respond. The right person will get in touch with you in due time. Provided you did not send a hundred emails to that same one and provided that when they do contact you (sometimes up to three months later) you have all your act together.

"Orly, that is all great but, when sending emails, how long before I follow up?"

Well, if you send an email with no response send a follow up email to check if they got it a couple of days or a week later. Sometimes emails go to Spam or to an anonymous email and gets looked at whenever. So, as long as it did not 'bounce' or an 'undeliverable' message received, you can touch base every other month or so. Also, did you notice that Speakers are last on the list above?

I live with this Mantra "Some Will! Some Won't! Who Cares? Who's Next?" I repeat that in my head as much as possible. Same goes for my Coaching Clients. We all know the saying. "You can bring a horse to water….."

Does Grammar, Punctuation and Spelling Matter?

Yes, it does. There is not much more I can say about that.
"The way you do one thing is the way you do everything." – Unknown

Also used by my friend and colleague Bert Oliva.
The way you write is not as important as how you write it. Yes grammar, punctuation and spelling matters, because you don't want someone reading your email to be hung up on your mistakes instead of your message. Same goes for you as a

Speaker. You need to be confident on stage and on paper and make sure you convey the right message in a concise and precise way. You need to work on your craft like Bill Walsh says. You are a work in progress. (More about that later)

So, if you do not apply yourself in the way you write, you will not apply yourself in delivering a great talk or treat the event planner with the respect they deserve. After all they are the real clients.

Don't I need to speak to the event planners before they hire me?

Not really. I know for a fact that event planners don't need to speak with you in order to hire you. I have been hired many times just because of my, availability, having my act together, responding in a timely fashion with relevant information to the items requested of me.

Of course, I had a conversation later, but I got a check first on many occasions.

So, is that another myth I need to add to the list of myths? Was that one of your questions in doing this business? Well rest assured, have your business in order and be consistent. The gigs will line up in the right order.

13
GET OVER YOURSELF!
IT'S NOT ABOUT YOU!

I must say the following statements are seriously annoying and so self-centered and self-absorbed and I hear them all the time. Most importantly, event planners are tired of hearing them too.

"I am a great speaker." "People love my talks." "I have no problem speaking in front of people." "I have been speaking for years, doing trainings and keynotes for ABC Company so I am pretty confident." "I have an Amazing message and it is so unique, it's nothing like what has ever been done before." And many more in those contexts.

Then, it happens - they get on stage and we, the Event Planners, are sorry we ever hired that speaker!
If you are a public speaker reading this book, guess what.... If you are not making $10K-$20K a speech and more importantly not being called back on a regular basis, once or twice a year by the same entity that hired you in the first place... You're not all that, so get over yourself.

Work on your craft and get real feedback from speakers that have been out there for a while who teach Public Speaking. Event planners are not interested that a few people in the crowd came over to you after your talk and told you how good you are. They are more interested about the people that came to **them** and said how horrible you are or how you made them feel.

You will never know how many complained or what they said, but you will not be back.

As a Public Speaker you have a responsibility to the event planner more then to the audience. So, you need to find a way to engage more strategically with your audience so that no one feels left out. And granted, some will, and some won't like you. But the likelihood of you getting called back depends on your effort on stage and giving your absolute 100% consistently. The way you do that is by practicing the right habits and by continuously craving feedback.

One of my all-time favorite World Champion of Public Speaking Darren Lacroix says, **"The Best Speeches are not written, they are re-written."** It is not a 'one and done' and certainly never perfect. (more about that later)

14

PAY TO PLAY

Many speakers I talk to on a daily basis are saying "I'm done with Paying to Speak" or now referred to as 'Sponsor' a speaking spot. They continue by saying "I want to get paid to speak, I am a paid speaker."

Boy, are they missing the mark! In order to explain to you why Pay to Play is a fantastic way to make money in this business I want to tell you a story. But before I do that, I recommend strongly that You Don't Pay to Play until you know HOW it really works and after you master the business side of Public Speaking.

The Story of Pay to Play

"I had been speaking full time for many years and about four years into my speaking career, a very nice lady that I met at a networking event came into my office for our coffee, one to one. In the conversation she said "by the way, I am doing an event for a bunch of entrepreneurs in a couple of months and I'm only taking four speakers. Each of the speakers will pay $2500 and they can sell their programs, coaching and anything they like and keep 100% of their sales. I'm thinking I will have approximately 100 people there and I will give the list of all the attendees with their e-mail after the event for follow-up. Would you like to speak?"

Well at the time I had never heard of such a thing as paying someone to be at their event and until that point, I have always been paid to speak. One disclaimer, I love exclusivity. So, when she said Only Four Speakers I perked up. She got my attention and a few minutes later I gave her a check for $2500 USD.

I was so excited about this opportunity that, I called a few of my friends one at the time, who are also speakers and I said this "Oh My God, I am so excited to share this with you. This lady came into my office and she is doing an event; there are going to be 100 people there; she only has four speakers and I am one of them; I paid $2500 and I can keep 100% of whatever I sell and she will give me the list of all the registered attendees for follow up. Isn't that cool?"

One by one my friends said "Are you crazy? You just gave her $2500 that means she is making $10,000, and maybe she will spend $1000 for this event. How do you know she will have 100 people? What if she has 50? What if she has 20? What if you don't sell anything?"

Oh my God, I went home from my office that day with 'buyer's remorse.' I was freaking out. I just gave her my mortgage money. But after 30 seconds of that huge panic, I thought 'wait a minute, I make more money than these guys and I have my business model intact. If anything, I will learn from this experience.'

Three months later the day came for me to be one of the speakers at this event. She had about 117 people there and I had sold only one of my Mindset Mastery Programs for CEOs. At the time I was charging $3600 for my coaching package so I, at the very least, made my money back. But it does not end there. Because of my follow up system and consistency, keeping in touch with everyone and following up with those who signed up for my Complimentary Discovery Session and another one of my processes for a FULL Year from the date of that event, I had made over $90,000 from that event alone. Nice return on my investment, right?"

I am sorry to tell you this. If you frown on Pay to Play or have a Naysayer attitude about it... It only tells me you don't have your act together; you don't know your numbers and you certainly don't know the value of Pay to Play.

Have you ever watched the show "Shark Tank?" Well, if you have not, it is a show that has 5 or 6 Billionaires called "the Sharks" sit in a room where hopeful entrepreneurs and innovators give their pitch looking for seed money or investment for a percentage share in their company. They may or may not get it depending on their knowledge of their own business and market for their product or service such as an App or even a membership site.
One of the "sharks" is Kevin O'Leary, and he is notorious for asking the question "what are your numbers?" You need to know your numbers, or he says, "I'm out and you're dead to me."

In public speaking it is no different. You need to track everything. How much you paid or got paid, how much you sold if you have anything to sell. What were your expenses and what was covered or not covered by the event planner, and how many people were in the room?

If you take my average of the example above, I made approximately $700 per person in one year. So, if I am asked again by an event planner to Pay to Play, I just do the math and then decide if it's worth it to me.

Now, I don't advise you to Pay to Play. If you have the money and it is minimal, such as a couple of hundred dollars and in your back yard then it is up to you. First, I suggest you start getting paid. Once you get paid you can put 10% aside every time for your Pay to Play money, so that when the time comes and you have mastered this business, you have your act together, and know your numbers, then, when a Pay to Play opportunity comes and you really want to be there, the money is already in the bank and you even know in advance approximately how much you will make from that event.

Now that, is knowing your business. So, don't frown on what you don't know. Educate yourself first.

15

WHY SHOULD I KEEP LEARNING PUBLIC SPEAKING? I HAVE BEEN SPEAKING FOR YEARS.

This one is a no brainer. The art of Public Speaking is more complicated than you may think. It's not what you say, it is not how you say it, but it is how you make your audience and the Event Planner feel.

You may have heard of this quote by Maya Angelou "People won't remember what you said or what you did, but they will remember how you made them feel." I am paraphrasing but to my point, you need to be memorable.

Not because you have a great Newsletter that goes out to your data base or message that you send many times in a day, week, month. Or you have a great marketing strategy. But because you are simply good at your craft and you seek to improve constantly.

Even Actors have to rehearse a thousand times their lines but more importantly they need to be able to draw emotions out of us, whether it is a jolt of fear, a smile, a laugh or a tear, it is their ability to practice their craft that makes them memorable.

Get coached, get feedback, write and re-write, practice and practice again and again. When you think you have it right, give your talk in front of a live audience and ask for feedback. Rinse and repeat. Continue as if your life depended on it.

16

"You want me to book You? Have you lost it man?"

This reminds me of Elaine Bennis on Seinfeld when she says, "Have You Lost It Man?" With a British accent. Makes me laugh, and so does any speaker that asks me to book them and they'll give me a percentage.

I regress. Every day I meet someone who wants me to book them as a Speaker and they will give me a percentage commission.

As I said before, there are only Two reasons why Public Speakers don't make it in this business: 1. They don't know how; and 2. They're Lazy.

And the number one reason why a Public Speaker will NEVER make it in this industry is that they want someone to do the booking for them. If you want someone to book gigs for you, you've probably been struggling for YEARS. We get that question all the time and it is annoying.

Our answer to these people is "That's why you're struggling. Yes, you don't have time to do it yourself. You're busy doing whatever's not making you money. Or you are just plain LAZY." And you want someone to come in and book gigs for you while you give them a small percentage.

Oh, and let's not forget to mention that you don't even have templates, a process, or any type of training that you can show them on how to find gigs and book the gigs. You just want to let them 'have a go at it' and magically get the gigs for you? GET A GRIP. You're not all that!"

My friend Benji Bruce says: "Imagine if Firefighters trained their people like that. "Hey, we want you to put out fires. We will not give you any equipment or train you on how to do it. Good luck."

Again, get a grip of yourself and your business. Take this business seriously or get out of this business because you are ruining the industry.

Nobody is going to do the work for you. If you keep thinking like this then another year will go by with you watching people on stage instead of you being on the stage.

Nobody can represent you like you do. You are the product. If you know me, you know I am a straight shooter and only want you to succeed.

I want you to understand something...

Yes, it's HARD. Yes, it takes WORK. And yes, you need to know what you're doing.

Building a business isn't for everyone. It's harder than you think, and anyone telling you otherwise is lying to you to sell you a dream.

I have literally done this for over 23 Years. Everyone wants the dream, but very few are willing to do the work.

I have hired most of the coaches you already know and or bought their programs and they are ALL GOOD. It is up to you to make it work and follow their program. Most people buy a program and 98% of them do not implement or even finish the program.

Do the Work, to Get the Results!

"Fortune Favors the Bold." – Unknown

17
COACH VS MENTOR

Speakers use these terms as equals. They are not and we are using the word Coach because it is common for people to understand. Let's face it, people come into your lives for a reason, a season or for life. They come into our lives leaving a thought, a feeling or a memory.

You see, thoughts are computer programs in our brain often placed there by people we no longer know or no longer care about.

The difference between a Coach and a Mentor is basically that a coach is unemotionally invested in the success of the 'coachee' and a mentor is emotionally vested in the success of the mentee.

Let's take a sports team for example. The coach has not necessarily played in every position of the team and is still able to help the team as a whole win a game. He has not necessarily won the Super Bowl but he helped the team get there and win.

Learning from someone who has done or is where you want to be is a Mentor. A mentor does not have to know your business but they need to have some business sense. They don't have to have the same goals or challenges in life. They just have to have goals reached and challenges overcome. You speed your learning curve by hiring a Mentor or a Coach.

Note: In this book I use the word Coach because that is what most people relate to.

When I first came to Florida, I wanted nothing to do with Property Management. I had been very successful in the business for 16 years and decided that I didn't want to do that anymore. I was the GoTo Person and admired by my peers. It is and was one of the things I was extremely good at. I met a gentleman Martin, who used to have the Largest Property management company in the State of Florida with over 27,000 units managed in 5 counties.

Martin became my mentor in Florida and in less than a year I had my own Property Management Company. In less than 2 Years I was the local expert on a local TV channel. And 4 years later I had published my first book on the subject matter.

This is from a girl who wanted nothing to do with the Property Management world ever again. I realized that Martin saw in me what I did not see in myself. Potential for bigger and greater things. He opened my eyes to the possibilities. Not only in Property Management. He opened my eyes to the possibility of making another dream of mine come true which is to help others achieve and accomplish more.

I started public speaking Seminars for the professionals in the industry that I knew well and fell in love with public speaking; of telling my stories of successes and failures in Property Management. My audience grew from dozens of people to hundreds of people. That is when I knew I had found my calling, but I was still not satisfied.

On a few occasions of my talks on Property Management, people came up to me and said, "you have such a great energy about you." "We love the stories and your personality." The one that touched me the most is when I spoke at that women's shelter, remember that story?

After some time had passed, I watched a movie called Pay it Forward and wanted to do just that. Be a Mentor to those who can't see their true potential regardless of their circumstances and events that have held them back.

You see....by the age of 35 I did not like what I saw in the mirror. I decided to apply a program that I had written on Mindset Mastery and take massive action.

I dropped the Victim Bag. I lost over 230 pounds and decided to take full control over my life.

How do you find a Coach?

First and foremost, meet with a few mentors or Personal Coach if you can relate to that better. Simply look for someone that you feel and believe has your best interest at heart.

Second, let them tell you their story and what they did to overcome the obstacles and challenges in their life. Find out what makes them unique. It is very important to know and like your mentor because that is the foundation of trust and you want to make sure that you can trust.

What you need to expect from a Coach?

For every individual it is different. It is unique to their own story, to their failures and accomplishments. So, I ask you to define what you want out of that relationship and then share that with your Mentor.

Your mentor may have some expectation of his /her own and you both want to talk about that.

One thing is for sure. **"You can't see the picture when you're in the frame." – Orly Amor** So, you need somebody who sees in you what you can't see for yourself.

18

WHY MENTAL TOUGHNESS IS NEEDED TO SUCCEED IN ANY BUSINESS AND ESPECIALLY IN PUBLIC SPEAKING?

When you, the business owner thinks of mental toughness you think Goal Setting, Time Frame, Task and Time management will help you achieve your business goals. That is how our business world has been trained to think for many years. Although this is a good start, you still need to take action. That is where the things you really need to apply can help you stick to the plan:

1. The WHY you do what you do?
2. Visualizing the End Result (almost like the business plan in Pictures)
3. A breakdown of action steps you need to take to get there.

Number one will define your passion; number two defines your ultimate dream and number three shows you the step by step path so that you don't get overwhelmed. Sometimes it requires a business coach to help you with one or all three of the above. You see, it takes courage and mental toughness to step out of your comfort zone. I am sure you heard this before "Courage is not the absence of FEAR, courage means you are willing to continue despite the FEAR."

Here are some of the questions you may want to ask yourself as the following are some of the questions, I ask my Clients to determine where they are in this business?

- How many times do you speak? A Week, A Month, A Year.
  - 1-4 times
  - 4-10 times
  - 10-20 times
  - 20+ times

- How much money do you want to make from your Public Speaking efforts?

  - $50K - $100K
  - $101K - $150K
  - $151K - $200K
  - $200K - +++

- What will make someone want to connect with you after you speak?

- How are you adding Value?

- How will you be remembered?

- How have you been getting speaking opportunities so far?
  - Through Referrals?
  - Through Speaker Bureaus?
  - Through an Agent?
  - Prospecting and Hustle?
  - "I am so good, they come to me."

19
10 TIPS YOU NEED TO KNOW BEFORE STARTING A SPEAKING BUSINESS

1. It's a Business & You **Need** to Treat it as Such.
2. You **Need** to Stand Out from all those who Speak on the Same Topic as You.
3. You **Need** to get over yourself. There are No Experts, Gurus, Rock Stars or Specialists. If you are the Expert, make sure you walk the talk.
4. You Don't **Need** a Book or a Website.
5. You **Need** a Good LinkedIn Profile.
6. You **Need** a Good 5-10 Minute Video.
7. You **Need** to Be Prepared.
8. You **Need** a Brand, Materials, Topics.
9. It's WORK! So, you'll **Need** Patience and Perseverance.
10. You **Need** to be Consistent in the Way You Do This Business.

The Industry of Public Speaking Needs Variety, Diversity and Women.

So, remember *"People Don't Care How Much You Know Until They Know How Much You Care"* – Sr. Winston Churchill

Strategize * Organize * Prioritize * Monetize

"Minds are like Parachutes they are both better when opened."-

Unknown

20

Biggest mistakes I see Public Speakers making

The biggest mistakes I see Public Speakers making are these:

NOT TRACKING; NOT TREATING IT AS A BUSINESS; and GIVING UP TOO SOON

If we don't know where we are, we can't get to where we want to be.

Conversely, if we don't know where we've been, we don't know how far we've come.

I see this funny phenomenon where Speakers are great at delivering their message yet are constantly broke or broken. They try getting booked and get either no result or a partial result and because they didn't get what they wanted right away--they abandon ship.

21
FACTS ABOUT THE BUSINESS OF PUBLIC SPEAKING

Multiple Streams of Income

- Speaking
- Books, e-books
- Consulting/coaching
- Royalties & Licensing
- Webinars/Podcasts
- Membership Programs
- Box/Online Courses
- Retreats

Platforms

- Corporations
- Associations
- Faith/Churches
- Non-Profits
- Government/Military
- College/Universities
- Education (K-12)

What Is the Market for Speakers?

- It is $100 Billion spent on business meetings, and events worldwide yearly.
- 23.4 Million Meetings and Events that occur each year in North America alone. That is 64,000 events a day that pay speakers.
- According to the NSA (National Speakers' Association), the annual income of a Public Speaker is $177K.

Speaker Fee Ranges

- Education/College/New Speakers:$1,000 - $5,000
- Up-And-Coming Corporate Speaker:$5,000 - $10,000
- Professional Corporate Speakers:$10,000 - $20,000
- NY Times Best-Selling Authors, Athletes, B-List Celebrities:$20,000 - $50,000
- Celebrity Speakers:$50,000 +

Other Statistics

- 98% of Speaker Sheets are done wrong.
- 1% of all the speakers in the world (including: Beginners, wannabe, part-time, full-time, corporate, trainers, politicians, athletes, celebrities etc..) are women. The Industry is starving for more women speakers.
- The median annual salary for motivational **speakers** is $107,173, which means that half **earn** more than this while the other half earns less. The lowest earners in this field **earn** $10,860 while the highest earners could **earn** upwards of $312,000 annually.

Here are Sales Follow-Up Statistics
- 2% of sales are made on the first contact

- 3% of sales are made on the second contact
- 5% of sales are made on the third contact
- 10% of sales are made on the fourth contact
- 80% of sales are made between the fifth and the twelfth contact

AND

- 48% of sales people never follow up with a prospect
- 25% of sales people make a second contact and stop
- 12% of sales people make more than three contacts

22
WHERE CAN YOU START GETTING AID GIGS?

There are industry conferences that pay a few speakers and keynotes. That's where most speakers try to book gigs without much success. Instead, a great place to book your first gig is by targeting Trade Associations and their events.

Since these are executives, you could speak on a wide variety of topics. You could teach personal development, productivity, wellness, etc. These are all topics that will help them as executives and topics they pay speakers to learn. There are a ton of different types of industry association events covering every topic. You can find one that fits what your business teaches.

You can also target conference directory websites to find events happening all over the world and pitch the organizer. There is no shortage of conferences happening daily. In either case, you can find and book your first paid speaking gig through these two places.

It's a great time to be an entrepreneur. Take your skills and knowledge to stages all over the world and add another revenue stream to your business. You also have the ability to sell from the stage or in the back of the room after your presentation. It's a great way to travel (if you want to) and get paid. Use this opportunity to expand your business!

As a Professional Public Speaker, "you need to be more motivated to solve the pain then get the gain." - Unknown

23
THE ADMIRAL'S SPIESTHE ADMIRAL'S SPIES

Five years ago, I decided to go on a quest to reach 4000 Event Planners that pay Speakers and ask them 12 questions that were pre-determined of why they don't pay certain speakers and why they tell speakers they have no money to pay?

I actually started with 5 questions, and as I was talking to them, I realized there are other questions I need to ask. Within the first few hundred calls I was adding a question at each turn.

I wanted to really find out the truth. Because I am sure you see Speakers getting paid all the time. So, my question is why not you?

I became obsessed even more then I have ever been before, because I was getting responses that were upsetting to me. Such as, "We don't pay Speakers," "Here is a Link to our Speaker application," "this is a 'Pay to Play' or a 'Sponsorship Opportunity' and here is a Link to find out more about that," "we already hired all the Speakers for this year," "you are not a good fit for what we are looking for," "you missed the deadline, try again in the Spring," "we hire Speakers from within our data base." This list of examples is endless. I also became super frustrated.

If you've been doing this for the past Five Years, you must be frustrated too. Are you?

I had questions that were firing at me like if I was in a war zone. I felt like shouting at the event planners that I was getting those responses from, "so when do you look for speakers? Where do you post your call for Speakers? How do you choose your Speakers? Why don't you pay or budget to pay for Speakers? How do you know I am not a good fit; you don't even know me?"

And, so began my quest. I have a data base that I have accumulated through the years of over 26,000 Event Planners (It's actually much bigger) that actively hire Speakers and I asked them to give me only 10 minutes of their time to ask them these questions. I promised not to share their information and not to solicit them for speaking, that this is pure research for my book.
Here is what 95% of them had to say:

1. Don't have their stuff together

Q: In general, what do you think about Public Speakers in this industry? And please elaborate.

A: Speakers don't know what the heck they're doing. We get bombarded with hundreds, even thousands of emails every day/week/month from Speakers who would like to get on our stage.

They send long emails that we don't care to read because we simply have no time. That is how we know that, either they're desperate or think that they are the best thing since sliced bread and still don't have their act together.

We ask for their fees and they don't know what to charge! We know that, simply by the responses we get.

Too low, i.e. below $1000 dollars they don't know what they're doing. Too high i.e. above $5000 dollars and not sending what we request in a timely manner, they think they're all that and really don't know this business.

Note: At first, you're not good at anything. Results come from correct application. So, the right thing to do, is doing it right. That is why I am so passionate about giving you this information. Don't beat yourself up. No opportunity is ever missed it is not your time. Now that you know, what will you do?

2. Sameness

Q: What is the difference between a good speaker and a great speaker in your own words?

A: There are so many of the same type of Speakers in this industry. We hear it all the time "I am a Motivational Speaker," "I am an Inspirational Speaker." "I'm a Leadership Speaker." "I'm an Innovation Speaker."

They all say the same thing i.e. "I want to change people's lives" or "what I do has never been done before."

We like to give Speakers who think they know what they're doing a chance and then they get on stage and they speak in a monotonous voice, or they read their Power Point slides, or they say what other speakers say and they use other legendary quotes to no end. If we are bored, the audience is too.

We know they don't know their craft and we know when they're 'winging it' and frankly we had to change our ways of doing business in hiring speakers because of that.

The one advice we can give Speakers is to continually get trained themselves. By going to Speaker Boot Camps or Trainings or Workshops with an open mind and an open heart, they might learn something new that they can apply. At another event they will get feedback from different audiences. Most Speakers think they're all that because they get praise when they speak. What about the rest of the crowd?

Note: Frankly guys, I prefer to hear feedback from a complete stranger that did not walk up to me. They too matter and you need to pay attention.

3. Think that their methodology is better or unique to most

Q: What is the one thing that is really annoying to you about Speakers these days?

A: They think their methodology, study, experience does not exist anywhere else. They need to get over themselves. Once we hear this type of talk, we look at their LinkedIn Profile and guess what? They are no different, they say the same thing as everyone who has or is doing the same type of work. 'Tomato', 'tomato'.

If they want to stand out, they need to show up differently. Think outside of the box and get us excited to hire them. Actually, it is also the reason we hire almost the same Speakers every time. Because at the very least we know what to expect and we know they'll deliver.

Many speakers think they're all that because some members of the audience have told them they're good. We feel that it has gone to their heads and they think they don't need to work on their craft anymore. We tend to call them Wannabes or Divas.

In our circle we want speakers to not think that. We also don't care about who and how many told them they're good. If they need to say that, to justify they're a good speaker, we know they're just desperate to get on our stage and we don't hire desperate speakers.

Note: Variety and diversity are seriously missing in the industry today and we are also missing women speakers.
"An ounce of Action is worth a Ton of theory" - Unknown

4. Don't respect time whether on the phone or on the stage

Q: What is your biggest pet peeve with Public Speakers?

A: OMG. Being on time and finishing on time. We are stunned by the unprofessionalism of some speakers who don't know how to keep time.

Note to you the reader: How traumatized are Event Planners if this is their biggest pet peeve? Think about it.

What you need to understand is the following as well:

If you are hired for a One Hour Talk, eg.at 1 PM, and if the other speakers took too long or finished over time and it is your turn and it's now 1:15 PM - guess what? Your time ends at 2 PM not 2:15 PM. So now you have 45 minutes. Deal with it. Respecting time is respecting the PROGRAM Time not YOUR time.

Get to the Venue an hour or two before the event starts, not before your time has come to speak. Event planners sometimes have to shuffle the program at the last minute and might need your help to fill in that spot or replace with your talk. Whatever the circumstance, be ready to serve. That act of kindness, generosity, flexibility and understanding, goes a long way with event planners.

Note: Go with the mindset that you are here to serve, not to sell. This will help make you the most memorable and get called back. I promise.

Remember, **"The way you do One thing is the way you do Everything." – Unknown**

So if you take too long on the phone to sell them on you, and you keep talking and then end up not getting hired… That is because, 1. You were not strategic about your conversation and took too long.
2. Which lets them know that you don't respect time and that you will do the same on stage.

5. Diva Syndrome

Q: When I say Diva Syndrome, what does that mean to you and what examples can you give me to explain that?

A: Calling, texting or emailing constantly before, during and at the event about all kinds of questions. We know they are not organized, and we know they are Divas, thinking they are the only person we need to deal with or cater to. If they can ask all their questions at once would be good.

When they get to the venue, we have assistants, volunteers, employees to get information from but they insist on talking to us. And the questions, are as follows: Where do I go to set up? Where is the A/V Person? Where are the Bathrooms? Who do I give my PowerPoint Presentation to? (If they did not send it prior to the event) Is it ok if I go a little over my time? Is it possible to have a bottle of water or Perrier next to me on stage? Will I have a small table on stage to put stuff on? Who is introducing me? Do I need an introduction, or do you just read my bio? Etc.

Another type of Diva syndrome is when they don't get their way. "Well you told me that I am speaking at 2 PM, why the change?" "I want to go first," or "I want to go last," or "I want to go before the break, lunch, dinner," or something along those lines.

Here is a good one: "Would you mind announcing that I have a table in the back of the room for those who want to purchase my book or talk to me?" Since when did we become speakers' promoters in any shape or form? They don't get called back and we don't recommend them to any of our colleagues. After all, we also look out for each other.

Note: I had a whole Chapter on this topic and decided to cut it out of the book. It was so long and depressing to read even for me and I am sure you're thinking, Seriously? Does this really happen? You might say this is not you. You might even say you're none of the above. But I am willing to bet that at any given time you have done one or more of the above. Not intentionally to be a nuisance but nevertheless, you have. We all have at one point or another.

6. Don't have a clue on how to treat an event

Q: What do you see speakers do at your event that shows you that they are not professional or lack confidence in their own business?

A: Oh boy! They show up at the event so last minute, maybe 30 minutes before they speak or 30 minutes before the event starts and that is already a challenge. They don't have time to go around and meet people in the audience and network like professionals. They are missing out on so many opportunities to make connections and possibly meet people that after hearing them speak might find a way to hire or refer them.

They sit behind their table and talk to other speakers gossiping about the event setup, the attendees, the venue and they are missing out on real time business.

To You the reader:

It is very easy to criticize someone else's work and efforts when you are not in their shoes. I invite you to do your own events if you feel you are better and have better budgets, clients, sponsors, volunteers and bandwidth to pull it all off while pleasing everyone in attendance. Please invite me to that party.

I have been doing events and paying speakers since 2006, and I have yet to have an event where everyone is happy. So, I wish you good luck.

On the other hand, you can choose to be a part of the solution. Help out the event planner while you're there; offer them a cup of coffee or a bottle of water. Go check the bathrooms and report to a janitor or hired help. Offer to present the next speaker or set up the next speaker for the stage. There are a multitude of things you can do at an event, instead of criticizing or gossiping or just sitting around.

Not organized

Q: You said speakers are not Organized, what do you mean by that?

A: We basically ask for information and we don't get it. Not only do we not get it on time, but it is either in the wrong format or even the wrong information.

For example, we will ask for a bio and a head shot.
The head shot is either their head cut off or cropped from a picture with someone else, or it's a huge file that we can't use, or it's a picture that is not HD (High Definition), even when we give them the specifications we get whatever they have and they hope for us to work with it.

The amount of work that goes into editing is ridiculous, so we will send them an email to ask them to revise what they have sent, and we choose another speaker because we know they will take too long to get back to us.

Secondly, the Bio is too long, it is a laundry list instead of a Bio. We feel that it is wonderful to have as many as 30 accomplishments, but at the end of the day, they can be just multiple accolades with a few as three examples. How they have solved a problem for others is almost never mentioned.

More importantly they either don't have a way to contact them on their forms or in their emails. If we have to look for it, we ditch it. We really don't have time to look for speakers let alone their contact information when we need it.

We collectively think that most speakers don't have it together. They don't have the right forms or the right mentality within the forms they provide.

Side note: 98% of Speaker Sheets are wrong or don't have the information or the content required to make 'a selection committee' choose the speaker.

Speakers don't get what a Speaker Sheet is or what is referred to these days as a One Sheet. Especially what it needs to have or convey to the event coordinator/planner.

To You the reader:

These are just a couple of examples of things that show event planners that you are not organized. Make it easy on them and you will have a better return on your efforts.

You might be thinking "that's not me," and I am willing to bet that you don't have it together like 'THEY' need to see it. You have it as YOU like it to be presented. There is a huge difference there.

Here are some elements to think about and work on:

1. Make sure your LinkedIn page is Rockin' – Description, Key Words, Videos, Video Testimonials, Endorsements, and an Amazing Banner/Picture/Head Shot.

2. Your Speaker Sheet is User friendly. – Contact info where they can see it at the very least.

3. Your Coaching or Consulting Offer is "Industry Value" priced vs what you want to charge or think people are willing to pay.

4. Stop working on your website or new book, thinking that will get you gigs. Of course, it is necessary or good to have. But lets be real, a book is a Glorified Business

Card and a Website is a Glorified Resume.

Don't get ready. Be Ready!

7. Think that they need special treatment

Q: Does it impress you when speakers name drop big names to impress you or press upon you to give them special treatment?

A: Well, it so happens that we can also name drop. We don't do it because it is degrading. Anyone that needs to say "I worked for Oprah" or "Worked for Tony Robbins" etc.... that means nothing to us. It is not why we hire them and it is not a plus for us to give them any special treatment. We hire speakers because of their professionalism, their message and organization, and, their ability to serve our audience.

Unless they can fill up the whole auditorium with Attendees or Sponsors, and we can sit back and relax because they know Oprah or Tony, then we need to continue working hours upon hours to make our events successful.

Speakers need to get off their high horse and let us do our job! No one is all that!

To you the reader:

Really? You think that who you know is a big deal? Or that you got to meet and take a picture with a celebrity? These days it is who knows you that is more important.

I get asked all the time "Do you know XYZ?" and I have never heard of that person. They tell me that the person is huge or a big deal. Well, that doesn't change the fact that I still had not heard of that person.

Do you know that some people around the world have not heard of Tony Robbins or his son Jarek Robbins? I did a couple of Facebook Lives interviewing a couple of these people because I was in shock. But get over yourself - not everyone needs to know those you know. It is important that people know you, because of the way you behave on and off the stage.

"Does a Flower need to say that she's pretty?" NO. She just is.

8. Sell themselves short and will do anything to get exposure

Q: What is it that you hear from Speakers that is an indication that they are desperate?

A: They don't ask what we are about or if we have a budget or if we have a way to get them paid. They just let us know immediately that they are willing to speak for No Fee and just get the permission to sell their materials, books, coaching packages etc....

We don't mind as that is one of the ways that we can keep our budgets low.

That is why we started charging speakers to be on our stage. If they are All That! They would not mind, but more importantly some will get into debt to get on our stage. Again, we have nothing to lose and everything to gain from this arrangement. We feel they are so desperate to get on our stage that they'll pay for it, instead of getting paid.

To you the Reader:

There are only 2 reasons why Speakers don't make money in this Business. 1. They don't know how, and we can't blame them for that. 2. They don't want to do the work. Such as study this industry. Know how to negotiate and get paid as a professional speaker.

Because You are Killing the industry!

You want more exposure? Go outside and the sun will give you plenty of it. Some people laugh when I say that, but I am dead serious. You won't get more exposure or respect.

I hear it from speakers all the time: "I speak 30 times a year" or more or less and when I ask them "Paid?" they respond, "no or not all." So, I ask you, why would they pay for the milk when they can get the cow for free?

I say to them as I am saying to you: You have come this far in your life. You paid with money, time, grief, blood, sweat and tears to get to where and who you are today. Why would you give it away?

This burns me up, because it makes it harder for speakers to get paid. No wonder.

When you decide that you need to monetize you have already put yourself out there almost to the point of no return by not charging for your knowledge, time and message. Now you have to sit back, learn it, do it and then delegate it or hire a coach to get you there.

Also, if you are selling from the stage or back of the room as it is also referred to and you don't make the money by selling your product or service, then you make nothing. By the way, selling from the back of the room is also an acquired Skill and unless you have it airtight you won't make money.

Start getting paid, then learn how to sell or how to not sell and still get clients from the stage. I do have a methodology for that and it would take another book to explain.

Just remember, No One can sell you like you can. There are no short cuts.

Like Nike says, "Just Do It!"

9. Freak out or get upset when things happen in a negative way

Q: What is the worst thing that has happened to you with a speaker and why?

A: We have had a few occasions when speakers got verbally or physically abusive. The reason does not justify their reactions, but we are sure that it happens everywhere.

The common reasons cited are as below (at different occasions of course):
- The lights went off during a presentation,
- Technical difficulties took away time from the speaker's presentation,
- We did not have their PowerPoint in our roster,
- We made a mistake on the spelling of their name,
- We forgot their preference of microphone, and
- There was a typo in their handout etc. etc.

To you the reader:

You might think this is not you. Just know that this can happen to anyone of us. You need to take a deep breath and go with the flow. There are a million things that can go wrong at an event and it is not always the event planners' fault.

If you are a professional speaker, then you know what you must do to remedy the situation whatever it is.

A few tips:
- Don't ever point or mention the negative situation on stage.
- Be prepared to give a shorter version of your talk.
- Don't make fun of it and make it look like it's by design.
- Working without a microphone has been done in many scenarios.
- Not pointing to a mistake on your name or a typo is best to do after the event if it is really that important.

Let it go. S$#t Happens!

10. Never say thank you /lack empathy

Q: Does it matter if a speaker does not contact you after the event and thank you for hiring them or for putting such an amazing event together?

A: Look, we feel it is common courtesy to let us know that at the very least, they enjoyed the event. A thank you is kind and polite and at the same time they can give feedback or suggestions to improve on next time.

We appreciate feedback when it is constructive and beneficial to the event as a whole, not that we should have or could have done things differently.

We do get a formal email from their assistants sometimes and that tells us that they are takers and not givers. They could not spend two minutes to write an email or send a card?

To you the reader:

There is nothing more gratifying to any service provider than getting a token of appreciation either by e-mail or regular mail. It goes a long way to treat event planners like human beings and not your servant. I hope you read the statistics at the beginning of the book - Event Planners have the 6th most stressful job in America.

I'm sure you've heard this quote before "If you're complaining all the time, you can't praise." – Unknown (I am paraphrasing)

A little something goes a long way. If by any chance you find a way to enhance their event before you get there. You will be remembered.

11. No follow up system in place

Q: What do you think is the number one tool that speakers need to have in order to get hired more often?

A: They need to have a follow up and a follow through system that is airtight. We see it all the time. We send out a call for speakers, with a deadline and they submit a day later or at the 11th hour.

They contact us to let them know when a call for speakers goes out and we let them know approximately when. You would think they would have a note to look for our email or contact us when appropriate and they don't.

We have a process by which we select Speakers:
- We pick from those who caught our attention early on.
- Sometimes it is just timing.

- We created an application that they fill out but at the end we might select randomly. There are just too many, so we might choose the first three that responded or more depending on the need.
- Sometimes it's who knows who within our organization and if they are available.
- We suggest that they submit an abstract, and if it is too long or boring, we give it to a selecting committee. That is why often you will see the same speakers at events. We just get discouraged by all of the above reasons of why we won't hire them.
- At the end of the day Speakers need to stand out and not sound or look like everyone else.

To You the Reader:

Remember, Event Planners have the 6th most stressful job. The thing about their job they hate most of all is hiring speakers. It is tedious and hard, and they have a million other things to think about and prepare for. Not only are you not all that but if you don't have it together, you're out!

Final Thought From the 12 Reasons:

"Good Speakers don't need to say they're an Expert, they just need to show their Expertise." – Unknown

24
LET'S GET TO THE 'BRASS TACKS' – MAKING MONEY IN THIS INDUSTRY

There is a difference between real and not real contacts when you're contacting event planners to get hired.

There are 4 things you need to have for contacting them through email.

1. A Speaker/One Sheet
2. Script for Event Planners
3. Script for Conferences
4. Scripts for Corporate Events

For example, I ask my clients to contact 50 event planners per day. Yes, you heard right - 50 per day. Only during week days so that adds up to 250 a week. My clients, using my system get an average of 34 to 56 percent response rate. Not hire rate but a response rate; where they got to the right person and if there is a suggested next step. If you are good at math, the average response rate is 85 to 140 responses. Because most of you are going to think that, "those are not good numbers" let me put your mind at ease - those are VERY VERY VERY Good Numbers if you know how to treat them.

Now what happened to the other 165 to 110 left unanswered? You guessed it - they don't count. If you did this every week for one month, you would have 1000 contacted event planners and have almost half not respond at all or very much later, like a month or two later (don't laugh, it happens all the time) and will you be organized and will you have all your ducks in a row (meaning your forms and things they might ask of you), will you supply those items within seconds or within days? Because that will determine you getting hired or not.

I have discovery calls at least 10 to 20 times a week and I love the people I meet. Once I spoke to a guy who, within our conversation, wanted to vent and complained that he had sent a few emails before leaving on vacation for one week. When he got back, he looked at his emails and one of them had responded that they were interested in hiring him. He got excited and contacted them back saying that he was on vacation and would be glad to speak at their event. The response was "we hired the first three speakers that responded to our email." He was livid and continued to express to me that he was in disbelief. My response was immediate "they don't have the time to wait for you, maybe you need to glance at your emails when you are away just for these types of emails."

When I tell you you're not all that! I mean no disrespect, but we are all here to make a difference and we are unique and special in our own way. "The times, they are a changing" and they are changing fast. Like Berny Dohrmann said "Super Change is happening Now" so, catch up or you will be left behind.

Unless you had 6000 real contacts with event planners you can't really complain that the system does not work and that event planners don't pay. They might not want to pay YOU. They will find a minimum of $50k if they wanted to have Les Brown as the headliner at their event. The only reason they won't pay you, is that you did not approach them in the right way.

"What gets measured, Gets Done." – Franklin Covey

Learn this Business, it Pays!

Conclusion

The business of public speaking is very different from crafting and delivering a speech. It requires, forms, systems for contacting and tracking, and a business model that is fail proof.

The mindset required to build this business is very simple. Once you have your Systems, Forms and Business Model for Prospecting, Contacting and Tracking your business, then, it's all about Consistency, Patience, Perseverance and Tenacity to hold on.

It's a Process not Perfection.

> *"Ability has nothing to do with Opportunity."*
> - Napoleon Bonaparte

RESOURCES I
RESOURCES TO FIND SPEAKING OPPORTUNITIES

Resources to Find Speaking Opportunities

www.SpeakertunityCities.com
www.Speakerhub.com
www.Speakermatch.com
www.eSpeaker.com
www.entrepreneur.com/encyclopedia/trade-association
www.SCORE.org
www.Vistage.com
www.SHERM.com
www.BigSpeak.com
www.MeetUp.com

And so much more…..

The point is most of events above give you exposure if you want to sell your book, product or services. Notice I did not write Hiring Speakers. They are Speaking Opportunities.

They don't pay but can keep you busy for lead generation and sales.

Also, Speakertunitycities.com is not only about finding speaking opportunities, it is also to find the events in your Local Market as well as getting you lists of Podcasts to be interviewed on as well as Radio Stations that are looking for guests on their show.

To get booked and paid you need to get to Conferences through Google and how you contact them DOES matter.

Resource - II

Here are some of the best Motivational Quotes that you might want to read when you feel down, discouraged or disappointed.

It's always down to you and the choices you make. Work on the things you can change and never dwell on the things you can't. You choose... 'results' or 'excuses' it's always down to YOU... no one has ever given their BEST and regretted it. GO HARD NO EXCUSES.

"No one said this would be easy, just know that nothing beats the feeling of accomplishment." – Unknown

"Turn those dreams into ACTION ...action turns into results... sooner or later you will be living the dream." – Unknown

"There's no substitute for consistency." – Unknown
"Once you learn to quit, it becomes a habit.... KEEP GOING!!" –

Unknown

∞

"Hard work can out-do genetics!!" – Unknown

∞

"Whatever doesn't kill me... had better start running" – Unknown

∞

"Our fears don't stop death, they stop life." – Unknown

∞

"Do it now. Sometimes 'later' becomes 'never.'" – Unknown

∞

"Kick yourself in the ass, or someone else will." – Unknown

∞

"The pain of discipline is far less than the pain of regret." – Unknown

∞

"I'm not telling you it's going to be easy... I'm telling you it's going to be worth it." - Unknown
"Tears will get you sympathy, sweat will get you results." – Unknown

∞

"Dear tomorrow, do whatever you wanna do. I have already lived my today and I am not afraid of you anymore." – Unknown

∞

"If we understood the power of our thoughts, we would guard them more closely. If we understood the power of our words, we would prefer silence to anything negative. In our thoughts and words, we create our own weaknesses and strengths. Our limitations begin in our hearts where we can always replace negative with positive." – Unknown

∞

"You can have results or excuses. Not both." – Unknown

∞

"You will never know your limits until you push yourself to them." – Unknown

∞

"Pain is just weakness leaving your body." – Unknown

∞

"I was not delivered into this world in defeat nor does failure flow through my veins. I am not a sheep waiting to be prodded by my shepherd. I am a lion and I refuse to talk, walk, to merge with the sheep. I will not hear those who weep and complain, for their thoughts are contagious. Let them join the sheep. The slaughterhouse of failure…Is not my destiny." – Unknown

"Good things come to those who wait… greater things come to those who are willing to work for it." – Unknown

"Set small goals for yourself and meet them. You are responsible to take care of yourself. You should be your priority!!" – Unknown

"If we're growing, we're always going to be out of our comfort zone…deal with it!!" - Unknown
"Failure does not mean defeat; to succeed you must fail first." - Unknown

RESOURCE- III
WHAT TYPE OF SPEAKER ARE YOU?

There are many types of Speakers:

Keynote Speaker –
Headliner or Draw Speaker or just an invited guest Speaker

Workshop Speaker –
Also called Training Speaker/or Breakout Session Speaker

Trade Speaker –
Speaking on a Specific Trade/Topic like a Financial Planner

Hired Speaker –
Usually is a Salaried Speaker within an organization

Lead Generation Speaker –
Able to deliver a Speech that generates Leads for follow up

Promoter Speaker –
Usually hired as a Hype Man to get people to come to another event.

RESOURCE – IV
RECOMMENDED READINGS FOR SELF-DEVELOPMENT AND ENCOURAGEMENT

- Super Change – Berny Dohrmann
- The One Minute Manager – Ken Blanchard & Spencer Johnson
- 7 Habits of Highly Effective People – Steve Covey
- The Seven Spiritual Laws of Success – Deepak Shopra
- The Science of Getting Rich - Wallace D. Wattles
- Overcoming Fake talk – John Stoker
- Dialogue Works – John Stoker
- As a Man Thinketh – James Allen
- Happiness Rocks – Ricky Powell
- Invest in Yourself - Marc Eisenson, Gerri Detweiler & Nancy Castleman
- The Richest Man in Babylon - George S. Clason
- The Magic of Thinking Big – David Short
- First Things First – Steve Covey
- The Tipping Point – Malcom Gladwell

- Building the Bridge as You Walk on It - Robert E. Quinn
- High-performance Habits – Brendon Burchard
- Beautiful Anarchy – David duChemin
- Never Eat Alone – Keith Fernazi
- The Old Man & The Sea – Ernest Hemingway
- The Power of Positive Thinking – Norman Vincent

Peale
- The Power of Influence -Mark Victor Hanson
- The Genie Factor – Jack Canfield
- The Millionaire Next Door – Thomas J. Stanley & William D. Danko
- Think and Grow Rich – Napoleon Hill
- 4 Hour Work Week – Timothy Ferriss

- There are no shortages of Amazing Books out there. I read one book a week and feel like I need more.

"Readers Are Leaders" – Unknown

RESOURCE – V

PLACES YOU CAN GET COACHING CLIENTS AND GET INVITED TO SPEAK OR GET REFERRED SPEAKING GIGS

- Associations
- Banks
- Business Network International (BNI)
- Career fairs
- Career MeetUp.com groups
- Chambers of Commerce
- Conferences – Too Many to Enumerate Here
- Corporations/Small Businesses
- Country/Golf clubs
- Dating & Relationship MeetUp.com groups
- Dating seminars & workshops
- Executives Network meetings/events
- Expos – Business or Trade
- Families Anonymous, Inc. Meetings
- Glazer Kennedy Insider's Circle (GKIC) meetings
- Groups at places of worship

- Gyms
- Gyms for women
- Hotels/Motels Associations
- Industry specific conferences/events
- Job skills seminars & workshops
- Kiwanis International
- LeTip International
- Lions Clubs International
- Marketing/Business growth seminars
- Marriage Support MeetUp.com groups
- Non-Profits
- Overeaters Anonymous (OA)
- Parent Teacher Associations (PTA)
- Parenting MeetUp.com groups
- Parenting seminars & workshops
- Places of worship
- Relationship Building Network (RBN)
- Relationship seminars & workshops
- Sales MeetUp.com groups
- Sales seminars & workshops
- Service Corps of Retired Executives (SCORE)
- Schools/Colleges
- Singles mixers

- Small Business Expositions
- Small Business MeetUp.com groups
- Small business seminars & workshops
- Spas
- Speed dating events
- Speed Networking events
- Sports clubs/gyms
- Trade Shows
- Toastmasters International
- Universities
- Vistage (vistage.com)
- Weight loss/wellness seminars & workshops
- Weight Watchers
- Wellness Expos
- Women for Hire career expos
- Women's Gyms

Resource – VI
Companies in the USA that Hire Speakers

- Abercrombie & Fitch
- Accuquote
- Ace Hardware
- Activision Blizzard
- Adobe Systems Inc
- Aeropostale
- Aetna
- Aflac
- AirTran Holdings
- Albertsons LLC
- Allstate
- Aloha Airlines
- Altria Group (Formerly Philips Morris)
- Amazon.com
- AMC Entertainment
- America Online

- American Broadcasting Company
- American Eagle Outfitters
- American Express
- American Greetings
- Ameriprise Financial
- American Airlines
- Amtrak (National Railroad Passenger Corp)
- Ann Taylor
- Apollo Group
- Apple Inc
- Archer Daniels Midland
- Assurant
- AT & T
- Atari
- AutoNation
- Auto-Owners Insurance
- AutoZone
- Avery Dennison
- Avis Budget Group
- Avon Products
- Bank Of America
- Barnes & Nobles
- Bath & Body Works

- Bebo
- BB&T Corporation
- Bed Bath & Beyond
- Benchmark Electronics
- Birkshire Hathaway
- Best Buy
- Big Lots
- Biggby Coffee
- BJ Services Company
- BJs Wholesale Club
- Black & Decker
- Blockbuster Inc
- BMW
- Borders Group
- Bosch Brewing Company
- Bose Corporation
- Bristol-Myers Squibb
- Burger King Holdings
- Burlington Coat Factory
- BMW
- Capital One
- CBS Corporation
- Chevron

- ChexSystems
- Chrysler
- Citigroup
- Citrix
- Clear Channel Communications
- The Coca-Cola Company
- Cole Haan
- Colgate-Palmolive
- Columbia Pictures
- Comcast
- Cool Touch Monitors
- Corning Incorporated
- Costco
- CVS Pharmacy
- Darden Restaurants
- Dell Inc
- Delta Air Lines
- Dick's Sporting Goods
- Dillard's
- Dippin Dots
- Direct TV
- Discover Financial Services
- DISH Network

- The Walt Disney Company
- Dole Foods
- Dow Jones & Company
- Dr. Pepper Snapple Group
- Eastman Kodak
- eBay
- Eddie Bauer
- Electronic Arts
- Elizabeth Arden
- Emerson Electric Company
- Energizer Holdings
- Equifax
- Estee Lauder Companies
- ExxonMobil
- Facebook
- FedEx
- Fidelity Investments
- Firestone Tire and Rubber Company
- Ford Motor Company
- Fruit of the Loom
- Gap
- Garmin
- Gatorade

- GEICO
- General Electric
- GE Consumer & Industrial
- General Mills
- General Motors
- Georgia Pacific
- Giant Food
- Gillette (brand)
- Go Daddy
- Goldman Sachs
- Goodyear Tire and Rubber Company
- Google
- H&R Block
- Hallmark Cards
- Harley-Davidson
- Hasbro
- The Hertz Corporation
- Hewlett-Packard
- Hilton Hotels Corporation
- H. J. Heinz
- Company
- Home Depot
- Honeywell

- Intel
- International Business Machines (IBM)
- Intuit
- J.C. Penney
- JetBlue Airways
- Jones Soda Co.
- Johnson & Johnson
- Johnson Controls
- Kellogg Company
- Kenworth
- Kmart
- Kraft Foods
- Lexmark
- Liberty Mutual
- Limited Brands
- LinkedIn
- Liz Claiborne
- Lowe's
- L.L. Bean
- Marriott Corporation
- Marsh & McLennan
- Martha Stewart Living Omni Media
- MasterCard

- Mattel
- Mauna Loa Macademia Nut Corp.
- McDonald's
- Mercedes Benz
- Microsoft
- Midway Games
- Miller Brewing
- Morgan Stanley
- Motorola
- Mozilla Foundation
- Mutual of Omaha
- Myspace
- Nabisco
- Nationwide Insurance
- NBC Universal
- Netflix
- NetZero
- New Balance
- Nike
- Nordstrom
- Northwest Airlines
- Ocean Spray
- Office Depot

- Office Max
- Olan Mills, Inc
- Pantone
- Papa John's Pizza
- Paramount Pictures
- Payless ShoeSource
- PepsiCo
- Perdue Farms
- Pier 1 Imports
- Pizza Hut
- Pfizer
- Polaroid Corporation
- Popeyes Chicken & Biscuits
- Price Waterhouse Coopers
- Procter & Gamble
- Progressive Corporation
- Publix
- QVC
- Quiznos
- Radio Shack
- Rayovac
- RCA
- Rent-A-Wreck

- Rite Aid Corporation
- Rockstar Games
- Royal Caribbean International
- Russell Stovers
- Safeway Inc
- SanDisk
- Sears
- Seattle's Best Coffee
- Six Flags
- Snap-on Tools
- Sony Pictures Entertainment
- Southwest Airlines
- Sprint Nextel Corporation
- Staples, Inc.
- Starbucks
- Starz
- Subway
- Sunny Delight Beverages
- Sunoco
- Sur La Table
- Target Corporation
- Tempur-Pedic
- Texas Instruments

- Textron Inc.
- Time Warner Cable
- Tropicana Products
- Tully's Coffee
- Tupperware Brands Corporation
- Twitter
- Under Armour
- United Airlines
- United Parcel Service (UPS)
- United Technologies
- US Airways
- The Vanguard Group
- VF Corporation
- Lee (jeans)
- Venus Swimwear
- Victoria's Secret
- Vizio
- Verizon
- Verizon Wireless
- Viacom
- Visa Inc.
- Walmart
- Walgreens

- Walt Disney Company
- The Weinstein Company
- Welch's
- Wells Fargo Bank, N.A.
- Wendy's/Arby's Group
- Westinghouse Digital LLC
- Whirlpool Corporation
- Winnebago Industries
- Whole Foods Market
- Wynn Resorts
- Xerox
- Yahoo!
- Zappos.com

Former Companies that Merged

- Affiliated Computer Services
- Aldus Corp.
- Allied Signal
- American Motors Corporation (AMC)
- America West Airlines
- Ameritech
- Amoco
- Apollo Computer
- Airborne Express
- Arco, or Atlantic Richfield
- AT &T Wireless
- Avalon Hill
- Bell Atlantic
- Bell South
- Chevron Texaco
- Cingular
- Columbia Records
- Compaq
- Comm Works Corporation
- Continental Airlines
- Esso (S.O.)
- Exxon

- GTE
- Lehman Brothers
- Merrill Lynch & Co. Inc.
- Nabisco (National Biscuit Company)
- NYNEX
- Oakley Inc
- Pacific Bell
- Texaco
- Universal Studios
- Washington Mutual

MY GIFTS TO YOU

If you bought this Book Digitally or Hard Copy on Amazon, and you send me an email with a copy of your receipt. I will send you the following as gifts:

- My Book: 1000 Things to be grateful for in a PDF
- My Book: 1000 Quotes to Live By as a PDF
- And a download video where I share with you the types of conferences that are looking for speakers all the time and what you can do to get booked in 30 Days or Less.

To Your Ongoing Success!
Orly Amor
www.OrlyAmor.com
www.orlyamor360.com
Orly@Orlyamor.com
Follow me on Social Media:
FB www.facebook.com/OrlyAmorcom/
LinkedIn www.linkedin.com/in/amororly
Twitter @Iamorlyamor
Instagram @Iamorlyamor

To be a Part of our Speaker Training Boot Camps Visit:

www.Speakertrainingbootcamp.com

Our Bootcamps include your Sizzle Reel

To get on our Social WOW Factor Cruise Conference Visit: www.SocialWOWFactor.com

ABOUT THE AUTHOR

Orly Amor is an internationally known speaker, business coach for public speakers, Networking Expert and author of several books. Founder of the Health & Wellness Network of Commerce, the Social Wow Factor Conferences and The Global Mentoring Center.

Soon after earning both MBA and Law Degrees, she dedicated her life and career to creating prosperity by helping others realize their own mission-based goals and dreams. Extensive experience as a Certified Behavioral Analyst has made her indispensable as a coach to many influential corporate leaders. Despite the impressive education and success as a businesswoman, Orly remains remarkably humble, authentic, and a very engaging speaker.

In addition to being, a great public speaker herself, and a great networker for the past ten years, she has helped Public Speakers create their Business Model for Public Speaking. Her gift is to show them how to monetize their craft by taking it seriously and having what she calls "Business in A Box for Public Speakers." thereby teaching them how to fish, increase their revenue and create referral partners through Networking.

Orly Amor | International Public Speaker, Best Selling Author,

Business & Personal Coach to Public Speakers, Founder of The Health and Wellness Network of Commerce Corporation, and CEO of The Global Mentoring Center Inc.

To hire Orly Amor for your next event simply call her directly at 1-917-515-6803

Email at orly@orlyamor.com
FB www.facebook.com/OrlyAmorcom/
LinkedIn www.linkedin.com/in/amororly
Twitter @Iamorlyamor
Instagram @Iamorlyamor

Made in the USA
Columbia, SC
26 February 2022